Fort Mellon
1837-42

Fort Mellon
1837-42

A Microcosm
of the
Second Seminole War

by Arthur E. Francke, Jr.

Banyan Books, Inc., c 1977.
Miami, Florida

CIP

I received the appointment of third Lieutenant... to deserve
which shall be the study of my life which I hereby devote to the
service of my country.

Charles Mellon, April 9, 1814

The soldier... is sustained only by the hope that his discomforts,
inconveniences, privations and hardships will have an end, and
that he will at the termination of his service return to his friends—
with the satisfaction that he has faithfully performed his duties....

Lt. John Pickell, December 14, 1837

Is not every act of the Indians sanctioned by the practice of
civilized nations? Are they not sanctioned by expediency and
revenge? Mark me—if in this unhallowed surface one drop of
Indian blood should soil your hands like Lady Macbeth you may cry
to all eternity, "Out damned spot."

Capt. Nathaniel Wyche Hunter, June 1841

Copyright © 1977 by
Arthur E. Francke, Jr.

Designed by Augustine DuBois

Manufactured in the United States of America

Library of Congress Cataloging in Publication Data

Francke, Arthur E   1912-
   Fort Mellon, 1837-42.

   Bibliography: p.
   1. Fort Mellon, Fla. 2. Seminole War, 2nd, 1835-
1842. I. Title.
E83.835.F73   973.5'7   77-11918
ISBN 0-916224-17-1

Contents

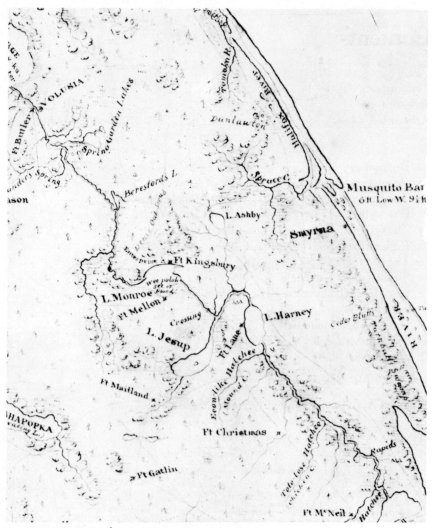

Detail of Army map L52b, depicting the Fort Mellon area. (Department of the Army)

Illustrations

Foreword

The importance of Seminole War records in the local history of Florida is being shown again and again, with the number of place-names the most obvious evidence. In a great many instances military men cut the first roads, established the first bases of settlement in the form of buildings, and wrote the first accounts of the site areas, often illustrated with crude maps and drawings.

These reports frequently go beyond descriptions of interest only to military offices and officials. The writers sometimes had an eye to a wider audience and recognized public interest in the Indians, the natural environment, and the potential for settlement. Occasionally their work found a publisher in a magazine of importance or, more often, in local newspapers or obscure journals; even more often it lay buried in the records of the war offices of the United States. Only now is it being sought out and made available to students and scholars and writers.

Arthur E. Francke's *Fort Mellon 1837-42* is a case in point. The story is, as he points out in the subtitle, a microcosm of the Second Seminole War. Students of military history will find some details clarified, some errors corrected, and some new information. Some place-names are corrected, and others are accounted for; with this begins the contribution to nonmilitary history.

Lieutenant John Pickell was a man keenly interested in all that he saw around him. During November and December 1837 he kept a daily account of all that he observed around Fort Mellon. Though Bartram had made some reference to the area and even John Lee Williams a reference or two, the first extensive account of the Fort Mellon area, which was to become the city of Sanford, is in Pickell's journal. In many other cases documents like this tell us all we will ever know about the earliest history of places that have since acquired a new and different importance.

The word documentary may sound formidable to some readers, but without reason. It lends authenticity and authority to the story. The documentary is now a favorite form of book, television, and motion picture presentation, and justifiably so, for the errors and folk tales that surround so many stories are thus eliminated. And what really happened in history, if it can be fully told, is always more interesting than any imaginary account.

We are reminded again that persistent and resourceful search in public and private records is always rewarding. Here is a model for the type of in-depth research required to recapture the past. The maps, drawings, and paintings of the period are every bit as important as the words.

Charlton W. Tebeau
Author of *A History of Florida*

Acknowledgments

In assembling some of my data I have had assistance from the National Archives and Record Service, including the Navy and Old Army Branch Military Archives Division, Military Service Records, and the Natural Resources Branch, Civil Archives Division; the Department of the Army, including the Institute of Heraldry and the Office of the Chief of Engineers; the Reference Department Manuscript Division as well as the Photoduplication Service of the Library of Congress; and the Council on Abandoned Military Posts U.S.A. I have been aided by the libraries of the following institutions: Duke University, University of Florida, University of Miami, University of Oklahoma, University of South Carolina, Rollins College, the State Library of Florida, Stetson University, and Tulane University, as well as by the Carnegie Library of Pittsburgh and the municipal libraries of New York City, DeLand, De Bary, and Sanford. Also helpful have been the historical societies at Tallahassee, St. Augustine, Charleston (South Carolina), and Erie and Crawford counties in Pennsylvania.

More particularly I want to thank those whose interest and generous assistance bespoke both goodwill and scholarship: Allen and Joan Morris of Tallahassee; Herbert M. Hart, Secretary of the Council on Abandoned Military Posts; George W. Rosner, University of Miami Library; Charles Walker, Historical Division, Army Corps of Engineers; John K. Mahon, Department of History, University of Florida; Edward A. Mueller, Executive Director, Jacksonville Transportation Authority; Dr. Dorothy Dodd, Librarian Emeritus, the State Library, Tallahassee; and Charlton W. Tebeau, History Professor Emeritus, University of Miami.

Finally I wish to express my gratitude to my wife, Shirley, beyond the usual words by which writers understandably acknowledge indebtedness to the devoted assistance and encouragement of their wives in preparing a manuscript for publication. Perhaps what I feel needs to be said is that, apart from the tedium of typing and proofreading, she always willingly offered to redo work the necessity for which I was in many cases the cause and of which I would have despaired to do myself. She was also an equal partner in deciphering the imprecise and florid penmanship on the maps and post returns and the material of the appendices.

NOTE: Copies of the two Vinton sketches, Fanning's battle report, Pickell's daily notes, Davidson's map notes, the maps of lakes Jessup and Harney, and the post returns have all been donated to the Henry Shelton Sanford Memorial Library and Museum in Sanford.

N.W. view of Fort Mellon   Lake Monroe E.F. 1837

Northwest view of Fort Mellon. Pencil
sketch by Capt. John Rogers Vinton. (Otto
G. Richter Library, University of Miami)

Chapter 1
Beginnings

We came to the middle lake [Lake Monroe], and...coasted
to the south-west or Indian side, which is surrounded with
pine-barrens, interspersed with some cypress.
John Bartram, January 17, 1766

The Sanford area made history in 1837 through an attack by Seminole
Indians against a U.S. Army fort on the shore of Lake Monroe. During
the three-hour encounter, which took place on February 8, Capt.
Charles Mellon was killed. Thereafter the military post, which had been
Camp Monroe, was called Fort Mellon, and the surrounding village
became known as Mellonville, both antedating Sanford but now part of
its history and within its confines.[1] This mid-Florida community thus is
located at the site of an important action in the Second Seminole War
(1835-42). Fort Mellon itself was active from 1837 to 1842, and as its
story demonstrates, Sanford's beginnings and history are almost as colorful as those of St. Augustine, though 275 years later.

Of the some dozen published per-
sonal accounts by soldiers and military officials who served in the Second
Seminole War, two are of particular interest to my subject: *Journey into
Wilderness*, by army surgeon Jacob Rhett Motte, and the journal of Lt.
John Pickell. The latter, who was an 1832 graduate of West Point,
arrived at Fort Mellon in November of 1837. His journal covers the
period between November 8 and December 16 and is almost entirely
devoted to the locale and environs of Fort Mellon. (My transcription of
the original manuscript appears as Appendix B.) Pickell's account brings
Fort Mellon vividly to life — no need to liken it to that other fort whose

account concludes, "Fort Dade is dead."[2] Fort Mellon has long been dead in the minds of Seminole County citizens; yet in 1837 it was very much alive, and that is how it should be remembered.

It is astonishing how much Pickell packed into a diary of about five weeks' duration — information typical of the war in general and Fort Mellon in particular. The *dramatis personae* were all present, as introduced by Pickell and others: both the military — generals Jesup, Hernandez, and Eustis, colonels Harney, Twiggs, and Fanning, the Second Dragoons with its band of musicians — and the Indians — Osceola, Emathla, Coacoochee, Yaholoochee, Micanopy, Arpeika, Coa Hadjo, Tuskegee. Other elements included the Indian "talks"; the Armistice or Capitulation; the Cherokee Deputation; the exploration of lakes Harney, Jessup, and Pickell and the upper St. Johns; nine steamboats including the *Santee* and *Essayons;* the deaths of Captain Mellon and Lieutenant Kingsbury and the wounding of Navy Lieutenant McLaughlin; and the ever-alternating hope and despair of ending the war. This was Fort Mellon in 1837. Similar events were transpiring throughout the territory; sometimes one event stood out, such as the Dade Massacre in 1835 or the several battles fought in the so-called cove of the Withlacoochee (the Lake Tsalla Apopka area in present Citrus County) in 1836. But the mixture was pretty much the same for the seven years of the Second Seminole War.

The war itself does not make for pleasant reading. It pitted approximately five thousand Seminóles against thirteen million white Americans at a cost of $40 million, more than the cost of the Revolution, as Andrew Jackson pointed out; and there were fifteen hundred white casualties out of forty thousand troops. Yet it is history — Sanford history — and should be told. Its lesson was not learned: like the Vietnam War it was undeclared and unpopular, fought conventionally against guerrilla tactics, and never cleanly ended. (One contemporary war correspondent employed a more classical description by referring to the Seminole tactics as Fabian.)[3]

The short First Seminole War (1817-18) was over before the United States had even acquired Florida. To oversimplify, it was essentially Andrew Jackson's northern Florida campaign against the Seminoles, who as Creeks had been pushed out of South Carolina, Georgia, and Alabama. Jackson's action not only drove the Seminoles into central Florida (thus setting the stage for the second war) but also frightened Spain into ceding Florida to the United States. His success made Jackson a popular personage, and he was appointed United States commissioner and governor of the territories of East and West Florida by President Monroe in 1821.

With the transfer of Florida from Spain, the Seminoles were anxious to come to some understanding with the new government,[4] which they did in 1823 through the Treaty of Moultrie Creek (near St. Augustine). For various considerations amounting to about $221,000,[5] the Indians agreed to stay within a reservation of about four million acres extending roughly from Tampa to Vero Beach and north to a little above Ocala. However, the eastern and western boundaries were at least fifteen or twenty miles from either coast. The Indians understood that the treaty would run for twenty years. As pointed out by Dr. Charlton Tebeau it satisfied neither the Indians nor the whites.[6]

In 1832 the Seminoles again felt the heavy hand of Andrew Jackson, now president, in the terms of the Treaty of Payne's Landing on the Oklawaha River near Silver Springs. This treaty, forced upon the Seminoles before even half the life of the previous one had expired, was the implementation of Jackson's 1830 removal bill, a law designed to drive all southeastern Indians into Indian Territory west of the Mississippi. The removal policy now openly espoused was resisted strenuously by the Seminoles. A third treaty ensued in 1833, that of Fort Gibson in Arkansas. Seven Seminole chiefs had been prevailed upon to journey there to evaluate the new country as a proposed reservation. Through sticky semantics their approval of the land was interpreted as sanction for removal of the Seminole nation, for whom they did not really have full authority to speak.

The government policy of Indian removal accordingly became the army policy of Seminole removal, which precipitated the Second Seminole War in 1835 and later developed into the doctrine of Manifest Destiny. Actually, it was the Seminoles' elusive guerrilla or Fabian tactics rather than any formal American declaration that initiated and characterized the war.

Pertaining to scientific data bearing on the beginnings of the Fort Mellon area, there are some recent paleontological and archeological findings coming to light at Stone Island on the northern shore of Lake Monroe opposite Sanford, where Fort Kingsbury (one of the Fort Mellon satellite forts) was located. As to prehistoric evidence from the Wisconsin Ice Age of the Pleistocene ending about ten thousand years ago, fossil fragments of sloths and mastodons have been found in the lake by Don Serbousek, an amateur paleontologist and archeologist and a professional scuba diver who is now working closely with the Daytona Beach Museum of Arts and Sciences. This same individual, along with Roger Alexon and Steve Hartman, in 1975 discovered in the Daytona Beach area, which is similar to the

Sanford area, a giant sloth skeleton that dates back perhaps one hundred thousand years; leading paleontologists term it the best and most complete giant sloth skeleton ever found in North America.

Closer to our time (being dated tentatively as about four thousand years old) are the fossil remains of three Timucuan skeletons inbedded in marl and found about ten feet from the shore of the lake at Stone Island. One of these, that of a woman about forty-seven years of age, was found facing downward but with well-defined rib cage, spinal cord, pelvis, left arm, and both legs, as well as a few scattered beads. This and the giant sloth are being displayed at the Daytona museum. Of a still later period, nearer the recorded history of Florida, are the results reported by the Daytona museum of archeological diggings carried on by John Raabe in three Indian shell mounds at Stone Island. Being unearthed here after careful sifting are parts of Timucuan skeletons and artifacts dating from 1000 B.C. to 100 A.D.

Thus the Fort Mellon-Lake Monroe area preserves evidence of some of the people and animals that were roaming Florida from prehistoric times down to the Timucuans, one of the six or more major groups of Florida Indians. The Timucuans, who lived in a large triangular segment roughly delineated by Jacksonville-Cape Canaveral-Tampa (thus including the St. Johns River valley), numbered about fourteen thousand out of the twenty-five thousand aborigines here at the beginning of the sixteenth century, when the Spanish came.[7]

During the English twenty-year interval (1763-83) between the two Spanish possessions of Florida, the St. Johns River was explored. This approximately three-hundred-mile northward flowing river runs roughly parallel to the Atlantic and wholly within the state; it rises in southern Brevard County (following for the most part an ancient shoreline) and is the largest and most important Florida river. The diary-report of John Bartram, the Philadelphia naturalist who was commissioned in 1763 by George III as his botanist for the Floridas and who was to trace the river to its source, ushers in the first English record of the Fort Mellon area. His diary discloses (January 7-18) his passage as far as Puzzle Lake (about fifty miles by river above Sanford) and back to the river just below Lake Monroe. He began his survey of the Lake Monroe area by camping at a "rocky bluff" (present-day Stone Island), which he described as "composed of snail and muscle-shells, endurated into hard rocks."[8] The Indians he met were the early Seminoles — not the Timucuans, who by this time were practically decimated by white man's diseases and harsh treatment. Immediately following Bartram's tracing of the St. Johns, another general survey of East Florida (1766-70) was made under the direction of William Gerard

De Brahm, the surveyor general of British East and West Florida. Later, in 1822, an American exploring and surveying expedition of the St. Johns was conducted by naturalist and officer Capt. John Eatton LeConte of the United States topographical engineers.

No discussion of Fort Mellon can be dissociated from Lake Monroe. This fourteen-square-mile lake shares with Lake Griffin the position of the eleventh largest lake in Florida. To the Seminoles it was Wepolokse ("round lake").[9] References in local land grant instruments show that the Spanish called it Valdez, by which it appears they were honoring Antonio Valdez, who up to 1787 served as secretary of the Spanish navy and had promoted an exploratory survey of Florida's naval store resources. It was reported by some that Lt. José del Río Cossa, a protégé of Valdez who was sent to Florida to conduct the exploration, made his 1787 survey in remarkably short time. As part of his report he included an enormous map wherein he changed the name of Lake George to "Laguna Valdez."[10] This is probably an error, resulting either from his haste, as observed by contemporaries, or from mistranslation, or from cartographic misinterpretation. It is also possible that the change to Valdez from Lake George was never accepted and that for some reason (yet to be determined) Valdez was applied instead to the Seminoles' Wepolokse (Lake Monroe). Sanford land abstracts have always referred to the pre-American name as Valdez; the Spanish also, somewhat loosely, referred to Valdez as the second lake or pond (Lake George was the first). Bartram referred to it as the "middle lake," but since Americans did not become acquainted with his writings until the present century the appellation was of no local significance. Another name that failed to take hold was Lake Grant, as shown on De Brahm's map of 1766-70, probably in honor of Gen. James Grant, the first English governor of East Florida.[11] The Volusia County map still retains the designation "Valdez" just to the west of the Sanford power plant at the outlet of Lake Monroe; and the Seaboard Coast Line Railroad maintains its Valdez siding into the power plant, having doubtless named the siding (in 1926) after the Valdez on the county map. At one time, also, there was a Hotel Valdez in Sanford at the southeast corner of Commercial Street and Park Avenue.

According to Charles Vignoles' *Observations Upon the Floridas*, the name "Monroe's lake" first appeared on an 1823 map, which Vignoles credits to the survey made in 1822 by LeConte. Vignoles included the map in his book. Since Monroe was president in 1822, it is assumed that LeConte named the lake in honor of the president.[12] Bartram referred to Lake Jessup as "the west lake." De Brahm on his map named the lake Beresford; however, this is not to be confused with the present Lake Beresford near DeLand.[13] Much later in

5

local deeds Lake Jessup was sometimes referred to as "the long pond." This thirteen-square-mile lake, only one square mile less than Lake Monroe, is the twelfth largest in Florida.

Lake Harney to Bartram was "Round-lake," just what the Seminoles called Lake Monroe. De Brahm's map shows Lake Harney as Lake Barrington.[14] The Bartram and De Brahm names for lakes Harney and Jessup were applied by men in the employ of the British at a time when Florida was British and no settlements were being made in the Sanford area; since there was no one to use them, the names did not stick.

By the dawn of late 1836, when Camp Monroe came into existence, the area that had been infrequently visited by the Spanish and English had become the domain for about two hundred and fifty Seminoles under their chief, Coacoochee (Wildcat). He, "made of the sands of Florida,"[15] as he liked to say of himself, would fight a new challenge threatening control of his beloved Wepolokse. On the shore of the lake, now called Monroe, he was soon to be confronted by the strong opposition of a wide segment of fighting men representing a new and expanding nation, whose citizens believed in a destiny that they felt manifestly held out the prospect of ever new frontiers. Yet the men of the new fort, named to honor one who fell victim to the accurate aim of a Coacoochee subordinate, did not necessarily envision their goal to be the same as the frontiersmen; the soldiers merely obeyed orders. Thus Coacoochee and his people were met at Fort Mellon by military men, some raw recruits, others officers seasoned in previous wars with England and Indians. A surprisingly large percentage were West Point graduates, fresh from topographical and cartographic training; one entertained a sensitive ability in and penchant for sketching local scenes. Some as engineers would build primitive roads and bridges to facilitate the movement of mounted men and detachments; others would practice medicine in an ongoing fight against fever and dysentery. One officer, whose detail was lake exploration and river charting, left us his daily notations of interesting events, of flora and fauna, and of Seminoles and their Cherokee mediators and provided glimpses of a rising new vehicle of war and peace — the steamboat.

Chapter 2
Pictures and Sketches — Camp Life

This place [Fort Mellon] of which I have given a sketch, [is] drawn
by my friend Capt. J. R. Vinton of the Army. . . .
                    Surg. Jacob Rhett Motte, June 11, 1837

Here the bed is the ground, with one solitary blanket to intercept
the heavy dew which falls like a drizzling shower during the night.
                    Lt. John Pickell, December 1, 1837

With regard to visual representations of the Fort Mellon area two pencil
sketches by Capt. John Rogers Vinton are of particular interest. This
West Point officer was at Fort Mellon from March through June of 1837;
his expertise as an artist is obviously related to his earlier army experience
in topographical work. The sketches are entitled "N.W. view of Fort
Mellon Lake Monroe E.F. 1837" and "Oseola at Lake Monroe During the
Armistice May 1837." At the lower right of both pictures Vinton placed
his initials. These two sketches belong to a group of five Motte obtained
for *Journey into Wilderness*; the drawings subsequently were separated
from Motte's manuscript, and only four survive: the two mentioned
above, "Indian Mound at Fort Taylor," and "Light House at Key Bis-
cayne." "Old Barracks at St. Augustine" is the title of the one lost.[1] The
four extant sketches are now owned by the University of Miami as part of
the Archives and Special Collections of its Otto G. Richter Library.
                    It may be noted in passing that
Vinton, during his stay in Florida, drew at least three other sketches of
Osceola. One of these was presented to the Seminole leader by Vinton
himself, according to the *Florida Herald* (St. Augustine) of July 8, 1837;
another is now in the Museum of the American Indian in New York City,
having passed through the hands of Gen. Joseph Hernandez. (Hernandez
noted thereon that he had taken Osceola prisoner in October 1837 by
order of Gen. Thomas Jesup.) A third portrait, this one a painting, was
sent by Vinton from St. Augustine (July 18, 1840) to his old Fort Mellon
comrade Lt. Christopher Tompkins at Fredericktown, Maryland; this
full-length painting and the letter that accompanied it are now in the
possession of Lieutenant Tompkin's great-grandson Christopher
Tompkins of New Orleans. These sketches are reproduced in a number of
books, notably John T. Sprague's *Florida War*, Joshua Giddings' *Exiles of*

Oseola at Lake Monroe

Osceola at Lake Monroe during the
Armistice, May 1837. Pencil sketch by
Capt. John Rogers Vinton. (Otto G.
Richter Library, University of Miami)

Florida, and Emma L. Fundaburk's *Southeastern Indians* (plates 284, 285, 288, and 289). Vinton noted that Osceola differed from other Seminole leaders in wearing his plumes hanging off the rear of his head; this feature is evident in his sketches of Osceola, which compare favorably with those of George Catlin, the most famous painter of the American Indian. Vinton also depicts Osceola with four gorgettes hanging from his neck, whereas Catlin's Fort Moultrie portrait shows him with three.[2]

A November 1837 arrival at Fort Mellon, Lt. John Pickell, described the Fort Mellon site in words suitable as a subtitle to Vinton's sketch of the northwest view: "on a gentle slope ... about 300 or 400 yds. from the lake ... and on the right and left open pine woods interspersed with a few live oaks and palmettos on the flanks." On April 9, 1839, Sprague was equally descriptive and a little pessimistic when he recorded in his journal: "The fort is a picket work and somewhat elevated above the lake. ... The situation is beautiful having a fine view of the lake and the opposite shores which are hung in the deep and luxurious green foliage which characterizes this whole section of the country."[3] Although he marveled at the sight of his men bringing buckets and bags full of oranges on board the steamboat *Cincinnati* before they left, he doubted that the area could be settled or cultivated for years to come.

The Fort Mellon sketch is significant in that Vinton included a steamboat—one can conjecture that it might be the *Santee.* At the right of the picture appear the pickets of the fort itself. On the rough sketch of Fort Mellon that Lt. Richard Peyton included in his map (see chapter 5) he inserted the words "breast works" east and west of what he labeled "pickets," shown as a rectangular shape rather than the usual square enclosure. At the southeast and southwest corners of the pickets can be noted the outlines of the projecting blockhouses. It is thus apparent that the fort was relatively unprotected toward the lake and that the main defensive effort justifiably was directed against the 180 degrees of land exposure. This rough sketch by Peyton is our only indication of how the fort functioned militarily. Motte in describing Mellon's grave said that he "was buried in an angle of the breast work as it then stood, close upon the margin of the lake. The position of the works being altered since, his grave is now enclosed in palisades."[4]

Drawing on the recollections of older Sanford townspeople in 1910, J. N. Whitner, in her little typescript history of Sanford, was able to confirm the existence of such fort buildings as officers' quarters, a commissary, and a bakery. There were about eight two-story frame buildings, one of which had piazzas surrounding both stories and a cupola from which signals were exchanged with the blockhouse at Fort Reid, west on the military road (Mellonville Avenue). The cupola might seem unique, but it was not—Sprague describes Fort King as surrounded by a twenty-foot picket work with blockhouses at each angle and in the center a two-story building for the soldiers, topped by a cupola where a sentinel signaled by ringing a huge cowbell. Sprague remarks that this device, though unmilitary, was very useful; however, the cupola signals at Fort Mellon seem to have been mainly visual.[5] Basic Florida forts must have conformed to the following general description by Woodburne Potter:

> The Pickets are made by splitting pine logs about eighteen feet in length into two parts, and driving them upright and firmly into the ground close together, with the flat side inwards; these are braced together by a strip of board nailed on the inside. The tops are sharpened, and holes are cut seven or eight feet from the ground for the fire arms. A range of benches extends around the work about three feet high, from which the fire is delivered.[6]

Still another picture of Fort Mellon (from a lithograph made by Greene & McGowran) appears facing page 268 of John Lee Williams' *The Territory of Florida* and as the frontispiece of *Florida During the Territorial Days* by S. W. Martin. This picture shows seven buildings and corroborates the Whitner mention of about eight two-story frame buildings. A similar view appears on page 5 of the April 26, 1963, Seminole County semicentennial edition of the *Sanford Herald*. The title of each picture reads, "Fort Mellon, Lake Monroe," and the open block lettering as well as the punctuation is the same. Also identical under the title of each, in parentheses and slanting script lettering, are the words: "(East Florida)." The *Sanford Herald* picture does not cite the lithographer, nor does it show what looks like a cargo-laden, unmasted, unstacked open boat to the left of the fort on the Greene & McGowran version; otherwise the perspectives seem identical, and the same buildings appear.

Since the two Greene & McGowran lithographs (the second is of a steamboat) in Williams' book were the only subjects printed by a little-known firm that lasted for the year 1837 only,[7] one can hardly judge their quality by the standards applied to such well-known firms as Currier & Ives. Nonetheless, the Fort Mellon lithograph is of great interest and real historic value to the annals of Seminole County. It is quite possible that Vinton's pencil sketch caught the imagination of the lithographer, although no artist's name is credited to the view.[8]

10

*A Florida fort with cupola, which feature
Fort Mellon also displayed. (National Archives)*

*Fort Mellon. Greene & McGowran
lithograph, 1837. (John Lee Williams, The
Territory of Florida, facing page 268)*

That the buildings shown by the artist existed as early as 1837 is supported by Jesup's order 10 of November 4, 1837, which authorized Fort Mellon to be reoccupied and specified that "the picketing will be repaired and all necessary Blockhouses and Storehouses will be erected."[9] Granted, such buildings must have been constructed rather quickly to be serviceable the following month, when massive forces were to leave Fort Mellon for the campaign to the south; but perhaps the lithograph artist arrived late in the year, after some buildings had been erected, and used his imagination freely. Since Pickell mentions only pickets and tents, it is clear that Vinton's sketch was done earlier in the year, and the authenticity of the latter's view is further evident in that it includes a steamboat (see chapter 7).

The Peyton map, in addition to showing how Fort Mellon functioned, depicts a wharf extending into the lake. William Vincent, Sr., of Sanford has several chairs made from lumber cut out of the remaining submerged piling of the wharf, which was removed in the early 1940s by City Works Manager Sid RiCharde, Sr., according to current city manager Pete Knowles. Although we are fortunate to have the Peyton sketch, the recent discovery in a private family collection of a complete map of Fort Gadsden, 157 years after it was built,[10] prompted me to look for other Fort Mellon maps. I had hoped to find further material among Vinton's papers at Duke University, but investigation disclosed no maps of or information about Fort Mellon. If the papers of lieutenants Peyton and Davidson could be found (providing there are any), they might shed some further light.

Ironically, the lack of a picture of Fort Volusia prompted H. J. Doherty, Jr., in his 1961 *Richard Keith Call* to show Vinton's view of Fort Mellon as a typical fort of the era. Both the Vinton sketch and the Greene & McGowran lithograph give us a slightly better picture of the steamboat than of the fort itslf. Because we have no physical remains and only a couple of sketches or pictures from distant perspectives, our image of Fort Mellon is a hazy one of gray pickets surrounding an enclosure. Better pictures still could not convey adequately the life of the camp; however, Pickell's account does give an intimate picture of life in and around the fort. Had Vinton seen what Pickell described in his diary, the pencil sketcher might have wished for watercolors to counterpoint Pickell's commentary, written from his primitive tent-enclosed scribe's sanctuary.

Tents it seems to have been for everyone from General Jesup on down to the Indians. The barracks were to come later. Pickell several times referred to the striking of tents, and he thought it a novel sight to view the Indians around their fires and in the tent they occupied twenty-five or thirty yards from his. Vinton or any

12

artist would have felt privileged to paint the scenes described by Pickell:

THE INDIANS

The Seminole chief Micanopy flanked with Cloud and Coa Hadjo on his left and Tuskegee on his right sitting on benches facing General Jesup in his tent for a "talk."

Coa Hadjo attired in the rich costume of his nation at the head of five Cherokee Delegation members presented an imposing spectacle riding slowly through the camp.

Micanopy and Little Cloud with twenty warriors riding under a white flag into camp.

Osceola's two wives with a retinue of fifty arriving in camp preceded by a white flag on an eight foot staff.

Seminoles around their tents and fires

Women cooking sofka

Men making moccasins

Boys shooting through the reed at small oranges

The dress of the chiefs and warriors with their wampum, leggings and frocks fancifully ornamented and their party-colored turbans crowned with feathers and silver bands.

Their dignified step and gesture

THE ARMY

The Commanding General's tent

The band of music belonging to the 2nd Regt. Dragoons arrived . . . and for the last two nights we have been favored with their music.

Left the wharf at Ft. M. at ½ after 4 P.M.

The command was forming on the grand parade

Reveille tomorrow morning

Court Martial: General Eustis President and Lt. Davidson Judge Advocate.

The Artillery and Dragoon encampments

THE TERRAIN

The ground a dense hammock, high, and with hillocks of shells, a pleasant situation facing upon Lake Monroe, a beautiful sheet of water.

One would not have to be a Vinton to be affected by, in the words of Pickell, "so many sources of interest . . . that almost constantly attracted attention."

Pickell's words "party-colored," "moccasins," and "leggins . . . ornamented" to describe his "red man" were used also by Washington Irving when in his *Adventures of Captain Bonneville* he described a Colorado River trapper as resembling an Indian brave.[11] The usage in common of the unusual "party-colored" and "parti-colored" may have been occasioned by an adjective in contemporary use and elicited by the always colorful Indian dress. It would hardly seem likely that Irving's book, published in 1837, would have come to the attention of an army lieutenant in service that year. In any event, this example of Pickell's vocabulary places him in good company.

Pickell thus depicts the brisk bustle of a military post somewhat softened by the then peaceful and colorful pursuits of the Seminoles — all on the fringe of the frontier. To the north was steamboat communication with civilization; to the south were the trails of runners to the Seminole strongholds. He also characterizes the duality of known and unknown, of old and new. He tells of bringing in an orange branch plucked on an exploration trip after having fired signal rockets the night before; a few days later he reports that "wolves for the last two nights have made much noise around our encampment."

From the short diary of another West Point officer, Capt. Electus Backus, who arrived at Tampa between the battles of Okeechobee and the Loxahatchee, we learn a little more about camp life. Backus' notes indicate that both officers and soldiers were quite often allowed to hunt quails, turkeys, white canes, and deer and that at one time a large rattlesnake and a water moccasin were killed. He describes the pleasure of receiving a cask of boots, sugar, and tobacco.[12] An officer indisposed with pleurisy was bled, but the treatment for men sick from eating cabbage is not indicated. Perhaps they had indulged to stave off scurvy, eight cases of which were reported. Backus also notes that he collected shells on the beach of Lake Okeechobee, as did Pickell at Fort Mellon. It seems probable that the extracurricular activities detailed by the captain were common to Fort Mellon as well.

After the battle in February Fort Mellon was on the whole a haven to the Seminoles. Motte's description of his relations with the Indians during his visit in June tallies with Pickell's later account. During the Capitulation the Seminoles enjoyed themselves at the fort, playing games and drawing rations; however, by December the Seminoles were gone, and the military campaign became serious again. By the end of December the army was gone too, except for a garrison of 184 men under Major Staniford within the large picket.[13] Thereafter Fort Mellon was a drab post; but when it was heavily garrisoned, as in 1837, life was never dull — not with such interesting people as Fanning, Vinton, Davidson, Peyton, Harney, Paddy Carr, Kingsbury, McNeil, Motte, Pickell, Osceola, Coa Hadjo, Micanopy, the Cherokee Deputation, Jesup, Eustis, Hernandez, Mellon, and McLaughlin.

Chapter 3
The Battle of February 8, 1837—
Camp Monroe Becomes Fort Mellon

We, last night, gave to his remains [Captain Mellon], all we could
give, our tears, and a "soldier's grave."
     Col. A. C. W. Fanning, Camp Monroe, February 9, 1837

Captain Mellon, after whom the post was named, was buried in an
angle of the breast work as it then stood, close upon the margin of
the lake.
     Surg. Jacob Rhett Motte, Fort Mellon, June 11, 1837

The story of the battle of Camp Monroe, to which Fort Mellon owes its
name, survives in four distinct accounts. The first of these is Col. A. C.
W. Fanning's report of over eleven hundred words describing what he
referred to as "the affair with the Seminole Indians" on February 8, 1837.
Fanning was in command at Camp Monroe, which had been established
in December of 1836 near where present-day Mellonville Avenue runs
into Lake Monroe. The attack by Emathla (King Philip), his son
Coacoochee, and Arpeika (Sam Jones) was a reaction to Gen. Thomas
S. Jesup's policy of more fluid maneuvering to encounter the Seminoles
in smaller units on various fronts. The chiefs hoped to surprise Fanning
and destroy the stores at Camp Monroe; thus a mutual basis of confronta-
tion developed.[1]

Fanning's report (see Appendix
A) represents our best description of the encounter. It appears in four
sources: the March 11, 1837, issue of Niles' Weekly Register; Lt. John T.
Sprague's Origin, Progress, and Conclusion of the Florida War (1848); J. H.
Eaton's "Returns of Killed and Wounded in Battles . . . with the Indians
. . . 1790-1848," compiled in 1850-51; and Logan U. Reavis' 1878 biography of Col. William Harney. Sprague was a captain in the infantry
during the Florida War and thus had a ringside seat. About half his book
consists of reprinted documents, most of which also appear in the U.S.
Congress Serial Set.[2]

Our second account of the battle,
scarcely three hundred words, is found in John Lee Williams' 1837 The
Territory of Florida (reprinted in 1962 as the second volume of the

Floridiana Facsimile and Reprint series). Williams spent a good part of his life in Florida: arriving in 1820, the year before the transfer from Spain to the United States, he was on the scene for seventeen years before writing his book. During this period he was appointed as one of the two men to locate the new capital. Since his book appeared soon after the battle of Camp Monroe, we can expect his account to be reasonably reliable. The omission of one "r" in Paddy Carr's name is minor; Lieutenant "Langley" is obviously Lieutenant McLaughlin, and Major "Harlee" no doubt should be Major Harney. Williams' description of the battle adds some details not included by Fanning. His book seems to have been taken seriously by contemporaries, for at least one West Point cadet, after reading Williams' account, anticipated that his first active service as an officer would be in Florida.[3]

Our third account of the battle, over twelve hundred words, comes from Surg. Jacob Rhett Motte, a native of Charleston (South Carolina) and an 1832 graduate of Harvard. Later he studied medicine, leading to his appointment to the army with the rank of assistant surgeon. Assigned to Fort Mellon to relieve the indisposed resident, Assistant Surgeon Laub, whom Fanning had praised in his report,[4] Motte arrived at Fort Mellon on June 11, 1837. He repeats some of Fanning word for word but also adds a few additional items of general interest to which I will refer later. (Motte's account was edited in 1963 by James F. Sunderman and published by the University of Florida Press under the title *Journey into Wilderness.*)

From these three sources — Fanning, Williams, and Motte — plus what we might term the Seminole minority report supplied by Sprague can be constructed the following account of the battle of Camp Monroe:

Brevet Lieutenant Colonel Fanning had been dispatched early in December 1836 to establish a military post at Lake Monroe. His forces, about three hundred in number, consisted of three companies of artillery, four companies of dragoons under Lieutenant Colonel Harney, a battalion of South Carolina volunteers, and thirty friendly Creek Indians. The day previous to the battle, these men had constructed at Harney's suggestion a two to three foot high picketing and breastwork on the southwest bank of the lake. Although Harney was aware that his rank and date of commission gave him seniority over Fanning, he waived his right to overall command of the forces in consideration of Fanning's seniority in age.

At about 5:00 A.M., a little before daybreak on February 8, 1837, the sentinel's attention was attracted by a rustling noise in the surrounding bushes. He barely had time to sound the alarm before a force of three to four hundred Seminoles under Emathla

16

and his son Coacoochee began pouring a volley of rifle shot upon the tents of the sleeping garrison, who also were awakened by the war whoop all around them. The Seminoles had surrounded the breastwork with a semicircular line whose terminals rested on the shore of the lake. In anticipation of a possible surprise attack, Colonel Fanning had wisely ordered his troops to sleep with their belts on and with firearms at hand; thus every man was at his proper post in an instant, and a sharp contest ensued. The onrush of the Seminoles was temporarily checked when they encountered the recently constructed breastwork, which their scouts had not reported. Their war whoop then changed to the cry *Tohopeka*, the Seminole word for fort or strong place; they retreated one hundred yards but continued to fire and yell from behind trees.

At one point the Seminoles dashed into the camp of the friendly Creek chief, Paddy Carr, and ejected the Creeks without ceremony, carrying away their baggage. On another occasion the Indians penetrated one end of the line of pickets. Fanning then directed 2nd Lt. George Thomas to go aboard the steamboat *Santee* (lying at anchor in front of the post), to serve its six pounder, and to direct his fire of grape and cannister so as to take the right of the enemy. This artillery action was possible because of Jesup's foresight, as evidenced in paragraph three of his order 36 (January 10, 1837) in which he had instructed Fanning to proceed upriver with the companies commanded by captains Mellon and Vinton (they being transported via steamboat armed with a fieldpiece) and to "be in readiness to cooperate with the Army if it operate on the St. Johns."[5] As a result of the *Santee's* fire, the defenders' flank was summarily cleared.

The Seminoles pertinaciously hung upon Fanning's center and right flank for nearly three hours and then fled, wearied of the contest, at about 8:00 A.M. They were followed by the Creeks, who mocked them and dared them to come back, but they quickly disappeared. Fanning, commenting upon the conduct of his rank and file, said, "Our men, being recruits, at first wasted a great deal of ammunition, and it was with much difficulty the officers prevented them from throwing away their shots. They soon, however, became collected and in the end behaved extremely well." (See Appendix A.)

From information given by blacks who came into camp after the battle John Lee Williams stated that the number of Seminoles killed was twenty-five and that a much greater number had been wounded.[6] In 1910 Mrs. J. N. Whitner interviewed Mr. Alexander Vaughan of Sanford, whose father, A. J. Vaughan, had enlisted as a soldier at Fort Mellon in December 1837. The elder Vaughan had remembered the blacks who had sought safety at the fort when the Indians had been repulsed and driven back. He also had stated that the

17

gunboat artillery greatly terrified the Indians, who believed it to be a thunderstorm sent by the Great Spirit to aid the white men. His recollection of the two boats present at the battle is correct, as we note that Fanning praised the captains of the *Santee* and the *Essayons.*

Captain John Lane's regiment (see chapter 10) was represented in the battle of Camp Monroe by Navy Lt. William P. Piercey, acting as captain of a company of friendly Creeks, and by Paddy Carr, the Creek chief, both of whom Fanning singled out for praise after the battle. Williams tells us that there were thirty Creeks fighting with the army during the battle. Paddy Carr was the son of an Irish father and a Creek mother; in the fall of 1836, he had offered to serve in Florida and had been placed second in command of a band of one hundred Creek volunteers. A total of over eighteen hundred friendly Creeks had assisted the army in fighting hostile Creeks in Georgia. Jesup, in coming to Florida from this conflict, advocated the use of friendly Indians and admitted that he had urged this policy in order to save American blood. Fanning said (see Appendix A) that Paddy Carr had fought well, had generally headed the scouting parties, and had performed his laborious and dangerous duties with great promptitude and cheerfulness. Fanning complimented Piercey by saying that "he is always foremost in danger."[7]

After retreating several miles toward the Ocklawaha River, the Seminoles met three hundred of their companions coming to join them. They were about to return to the battle when a runner from the top Seminole chief, Micanopy, informed them of the Armistice or Capitulation, negotiations for which were then in process, though it was not formally signed until March 6. Emathla was believed to be badly wounded, as he had not been seen since the battle, and the Indians were saying that he was sick. Fanning, on examining the battleground, found no dead enemies. He did observe several trails apparently made by the dragging off of dead bodies; he also found several belts and straps covered with blood, a small pouch of bullets, and some scalping knives.

Although the number of Seminoles killed exceeded that of the defenders, Fanning regretted the loss of Captain Mellon of the Second Regiment of Artillery, the only fatality. Mellon fell dead at his post a few minutes after the combat commenced, having received a ball in his breast. One of Coacoochee's subchiefs later boasted that, creeping upon his hands and knees near to the breastwork and lying behind a tree, he had killed an officer passing a gap in the breastwork. (See chapter 10 for biographical information about Captain Mellon and the other officers whom Fanning commended after the battle.) The only officer wounded was Passed-Midshipman John

Coacoochee (Wildcat). Oil portrait by James Hutchinson. (Courtesy of the Hutchinson House Press, Inc.)

McLaughlin of the navy, who had been serving as an aide to Colonel Fanning and who was incapacitated for nineteen months. The total wounded including McLaughlin was fifteen.

Surgeon Motte adds one adventure that occurred two nights before the attack was made: He relates how lieutenants McLaughlin and Thomas took an afternoon horseback ride that ended in their being discovered by Indians. The two officers spent the night hiding in the palmetto without their mounts and finally crawled back to camp in daylight. Their outing seemed foolhardy, but it did alert the camp that there were many Indians in the vicinity.

According to Sprague's Seminole version, Arpeika had instigated the attack, fired the first shot, and left Coacoochee with two hundred warriors to fight the battle. The attack was made just at the break of day. The Indians were surprised at the strength of the enemy, as their scouts the day before had reported fewer numbers (a detachment of artillery had arrived the afternoon previous); nevertheless, they determined to carry the place by assault, but on approaching they found the post protected by the extensive breastwork. Coacoochee recalled that his forces had maintained a continual stream of fire. He reported that one of his chiefs had killed Captain Mellon and that he had three men killed and wounded. Ultimately, the Indians withdrew and retired to the Ocklawaha River.[8]

(Although Coacoochee is usually pictured as a fierce fighter, he also showed a definite affinity for necromancy. This interest in communication with the departed was centered in the memory of his beloved twin sister, whose spirit he felt to be his guardian angel and inspiration. During the battle of Camp Monroe he claimed that he heard her voice, which sounded like the moaning of a dove and seemed to be saying, "Come, come, come.")[9]

After the battle Fanning notes that he was given instructions to cease hostilities and fall back upon Volusia (across the river from present day Astor in Lake County), doubtless in compliance with the spirit of the Armistice of which Micanopy appraised the Seminoles after the battle. On February 12 Fanning was at Fort Call (Volusia); he reported to Jesup that after arriving at Camp Monroe on January 29 "with ample supplies for your army," he was attacked by the enemy in great force on February 8. He further stated that the enemy was repulsed and did not show himself afterward. Fanning then explained that on the ninth he had received Jesup's orders to retire to Fort Call and that he could have arrived there by the tenth but that he "deferred the retrograde motion until this morning, not willing the enemy should think we retired in consequence of the contest with him." He included a copy of his official report to the

20

adjutant general and also a copy of an order read at the grave of the late Captain Mellon, of which he hoped that Jesup would approve and which reads as follows (note Fanning's misspelling of Monroe):

Camp Munroe
11th Febry. 1837

Detachment Order.

We are now under Arms to pay the last rites to the mortal remains of a brave man and good soldier. Capt. Mellon served during the last war with Great Britian. Subsequently, he distinguished himself in the bloody affair of the Wislacoochie; and finally, on this spot, gave up his life to his country. Honor to his memory! Henceforth, the strong picket work constructed here by your labor, will be called Fort Mellon.

A. C. W. Fanning
Bvt. Lt. Col. Comdg. Detachment[10]

The date of this order might dictate that February 11, rather than February 8, be observed as Founder's Day in Sanford.

On one point of the Camp Monroe Seminole affair Fanning and Motte differ: Motte identified the attacking force as "six hundred blood thirsty Micasukies," but Fanning, who would have known better than anyone else, figured the number at three to four hundred, with which estimate Jesup concurred on the basis of information revealed to him by later intelligence. (Sprague states that the forces under Coacoochee numbered two hundred.) Fanning's own forces numbered over three hundred, the post returns for March as well as February showing an aggregate of 364. This included the Second Dragoons, who had arrived on February 6, thus invalidating the Seminole spies' report that there were not more than one hundred soldiers in camp.[11]

Whether, as has been stated, the battle of Camp Monroe (also referred to as the battle of Fort Mellon) was one of the fiercest is debatable. The loss of over one hundred at the Dade massacre might be better so described, or the battle of Okeechobee, which has been called the severest, the greatest, and the hardest.[12] The use of a cannon was not unique, as Dade's men the year before had dragged one along with them through the woods; and even the firing of cannon from a vessel, although probably unique to the Camp Monroe affair (unless we consider the cannon shot from an armed vessel on the Apalachicola in 1816, which by luck destroyed the powder magazine of Negro Fort), established no precedent, because battles were fought where the Indians were found, which seldom was

21

on navigable waters. The effectiveness of cannon against Indians had been shown before; this was just one more demonstration that the army's presence would be increasingly and unrelentingly felt.

This assessment may somewhat diminish the glory so often claimed by the battle's adulatory chroniclers. However, other events, independent of the battle, make for an interesting and colorful local history that often mirrors the overall history of the Second Seminole War. In other words, the story of Fort Mellon is much more than the battle itself.

Chapter 4
The Capitulation –
Summer Slowdown

I have allowed them liberal terms, in which I have consulted good policy as well as humanity.

Gen. Thomas S. Jesup, March 7, 1837

The garrison has been withdrawn from...Fort Mellon...during the sickly season.

Gen. Thomas S. Jesup, June 24, 1837

We have seen that the Seminoles and the army both pulled back and ceased military activity after the battle at Camp Monroe. This cessation was in accordance with a formal understanding. "Capitulation" was the title of the eleven-article agreement that General Jesup and five Seminole chiefs signed at Fort Drane near the Withlacoochee River on March 6, 1837. More popularly referred to as the Armistice, it was brought about by mutual interests. (Both sides were always ready to end the war, albeit on their own terms, so that the hostilities were punctuated by many "talks.") The harassed Seminoles, having been engrossed in warfare, needed time to plant corn, potatoes, and pumpkins for the coming season, while Jesup saw the Armistice as a new opportunity to negotiate in council for removal of the Seminoles to the West. However, he was taking no chances: in a dispatch dated March 15, 1837, he "directed Lieutenant Colonel Harney to reoccupy Fort Mellon, on Lake Monroe, and build storehouses and collect supplies, so that in the event of the renewal of hostilities, I shall be able to move into the heart of the enemy's country, and remain there."[1]

Article 5 was the principal point achieved by the Indians and the principal concession Jesup had to make. By this article the blacks of the Seminoles were considered their allies and their bona fide property and could accompany them to the West. This provision attests to the strength of black influence in Seminole councils, especially that of Abraham, who knew that without such legal protection the black cause would be lost. The blacks, mostly runaway slaves, were held in a type of semiservitude because of their valuable assets, such as their knowledge of agriculture and the white man's language. Since their freedom was at stake the blacks fought side by side with the Seminoles. To the slaveholders Article 5 meant the emancipation of all slaves who had fled and joined the Seminoles to take up arms. Jesup soon began to feel the pressure of the slaveholders on this point, and he gradually modified his treaty position.[2]

In the spring of 1837 the Seminoles were taking the Capitulation seriously. A spot within ten miles of Fort Brooke (Tampa Bay) was agreed upon as the assembly point, and by the middle of May Halpatter (Alligator), Holatoochee, Ote Emathla (Jumper), Yaholoochee (Cloud), and occasionally Coacoochee had congregated there. Along the St. Johns, however, the Seminoles gathered at Fort Mellon. Jesup in a message (May 8, 1837) to Secretary of War Joel Roberts Poinsett[3] quoted Harney, who was in command at Fort Mellon, as saying that Coa Hadjo was encamped about twenty miles from Fort Mellon and Osceola about fifteen miles away from the fort. Harney further stated that "Powell [Osceola] slept in my tent last night with me."[4] Estimates of the number at Fort Mellon were put at about twenty-five hundred, and Indian encampments were spread over a radius of twenty miles around the fort; the chiefs included Osceola, Arpeika, Coa Hadjo, Tuskeneha, Emathla, and Coacoochee. For entertainment and to bring in the scattered Seminoles a great lacrosse game was held at Fort Mellon early in May (Osceola is credited with its sponsorship) to which the officers of the fort were invited as spectators.[5]

It is unfortunate for Osceola that he apparently was not familiar with the stratagem used by the Chippewas during Pontiac's Conspiracy in 1763 at Fort Michilimackinac. The British garrison there had also been invited to watch a lacrosse game in front of the fort. During the game the ball was tossed through the fort's open gate; the players then broke for the sidelines where the squaws were concealing weapons under blankets, and armed with deadlier instruments than their sticks they followed the ball into the fort, which they took over.[6] But Osceola seems to have liked lacrosse, for he came prepared to play just before his capture later in the year. He resorted to other devices for his strategic moves.

24

In the first week of May, Colonel Harney was confident that it would not be more than a week before the Seminoles were all on the road to Tampa Bay, as Osceola and Coa Hadjo assured him — in fact, it was pointed out they were encamped near Fort Mellon on the road to Tampa and that only a little indulgence was required.[7] However, instead of leaving for Fort Brooke, where twenty-six vessels were waiting for the embarkation to New Orleans, the Seminoles remained near Fort Mellon until the middle of June, drawing rations that according to the Capitulation were not to start until they gathered near Fort Brooke.

It is interesting to find the camps of some of these visitors indicated on the Peyton and Davidson maps of Fort Mellon that were recently uncovered at the National Archives (see chapter 5). Osceola ("Powell") is located by Davidson near the southern end of Lake Harney on the St. Augustine Trail (where it met another trail to Fort Mellon) and a little north of the Econlockhatchee ("Econlaik Hatchee"). Coa Hadjo ("Coe Hajo"), Arpeika ("Sam Jones"), and "Hoithleepoya" are indicated a little to the east of Osceola near the Little Econlockhatchee and a trail to Fort Mellon. Although "Hoithleepoya" could conceivably be the "Hoith-lee-ma-tee" who signed the Capitulation and the Treaty of Payne's Landing, John Lee Williams is almost certainly right to identify the latter as Ote Emathla (Jumper).[8] Unfortunately, the name "Hoithleepoya" seems not to have survived in any other records or accounts. About halfway between Lake Monroe and Lake Harney, near where the St. Augustine Trail crossed the St. Johns, Davidson shows the Yuchis ("Uchees"), who were followers of Yuchi Billy. Peyton locates "Euchee Billy" on the south shore of Lake Jessup in the "old field" almost opposite Circle Island, while near the western end of Lake Jessup he shows the "supposed position of Coa-Hajo's and Arpeicka's camps."

Another interesting Indian name can be noted on Davidson's map, although the reference is not to a person but to a town. At the "crossing" of Lake Jessup Davidson shows a trail going west "to Ahapopka." This name, now shortened to Apopka, comes from the Creek words *aha*, "potato," and *popka*, "eating place."[9]

Peyton's notation "camping grounds where the Negroes surrendered" may refer to the "twelve at Fort Mellon" listed by Jesup among the ninety Indian blacks whom he reported in June as captured. Jesup also later reported that "fifty-four Indians and Negroes surrendered at Fort Mellon in November."[10] Blacks were the subject of numerous messages sent from Jesup to Harney during March, April, and May at Fort Mellon. These communications reflect Jesup's gradual modification of Article 5: he first ordered the Seminoles to send all slaves taken from white people during the war to Fort Mellon and Volusia and finally permitted citizens to visit any of the posts on the St. Johns in quest of escaped slaves. On May 25 Jesup wrote Harney the letter that first introduced the subject of importing bloodhounds (in 1840 actually employed by Zachary Taylor, much to the dismay of some members of Congress):

> If you see Powell again, I wish you to tell him that I intend to send exploring and surveying parties into every part of the country during the summer, and that I shall send out and take all the negroes who belong to the white people, and he must not allow the Indians or Indian negroes to mix with them. Tell him I am sending to Cuba for bloodhounds to trail them, and I intend to hang every one of them who does not come in.[11]

Joshua Giddings, the abolitionist, sees this as the cause of the collapse of the Capitulation. The clincher came early in June when Osceola and Arpeika left Fort Mellon for Tampa where by force they cleared out about seven hundred Indians at Fort Brooke waiting embarkation to New Orleans.[12] Thus the "Capitulation which might have taken its place among the important documents of the country was doomed to be forgotten."[13]

This account of the Capitulation provides background for the Vinton sketch of Osceola at Fort Mellon and documents the Indian references on the Peyton and Davidson maps. The maps, in turn, provide a new historical background for the Capitulation and substantiate its written record, which was the only previous evidence. The story of the Capitulation also underlines Fort Mellon's position as the site of the Seminole encampments and as the receiving station for the communications that Jesup sent to Harney on the subject of runaway slaves.

We recall that Surgeon Motte had been instructed by General Jesup to proceed to Fort Mellon in order to relieve the indisposed Dr. Laub. Motte pointed out that the extreme sickness among the troops there necessitated the constant attendance of a physician. This condition was not peculiar to Fort Mellon but affected all posts in Florida, especially in summer. Motte had observed the same situation at Volusia, which he referred to as a miasmatic region. Sprague pointed out that summer was the Indians' ally and claimed that the prevailing disease was dysentery, caused by the soldiers' being obliged to drink turbid water from stagnant ponds.[14] Many referred to this time as the sickly season.

Such was the situation at Fort

Mellon when Motte arrived on June 11, 1837. He was heartened to renew acquaintances with Paddy Carr and his band of Creek warriors, Lieutenant Peyton, and possibly Captain Vinton.[15] (Perhaps at this time Motte first became acquainted with Vinton's pencil sketches.) Next morning, however, the surgeon found a sick list of over seventy awaiting him at the hospital, a strong argument in favor of immediate abandonment of the post. In fact, Colonel Harney had already received orders to withdraw; Motte said the commandant had boldly delayed so as to try out some new plan of his for catching the Seminoles. Motte compared the plan with the infeasibility of catching birds by putting salt on their tails.

Motte noted that during the time of truce the Seminoles were constantly coming into camp and fraternizing with Paddy Carr and his Creeks. Coacoochee was a constant visitor to the tent of the doctor and took special pleasure in Motte's superfine port wine medicine. The surgeon also observed the frequent "ball plays between the Creeks and Seminoles; and among the former alone. Back of our camp there was a wide level plain, the scene of these exercises; where several hundred Indians might every day have been seen, quite naked, enjoying their favorite amusement." A "ball play," as described by William Bartram in his *Travels*, is the game later adopted and named lacrosse.[16]

On the serious side, Motte noted that Lt. Charles E. Kingsbury of the Second Dragoons had been buried the day before the surgeon arrived. Kingsbury was one of the officers cited by Colonel Fanning after the battle of Camp Monroe. In Sprague's appendix to *The Florida War*, Kingsbury is said to have died of fever near Fort Mellon on June 9, 1837, after serving a year and a day in the army. Motte's statement that Kingsbury had been buried on the tenth confirms Sprague's testimony.[17]

Kingsbury's name was given to one of the Fort Mellon satellite forts. When the Stone Island community development was undertaken about 1970 on the northeastern shore of Lake Monroe, a land survey revealed that Fort Kingsbury had been located about where the skeet range is shown on the developer's site map. It was further revealed that this fort had been in active service for only about six weeks as a rest and work camp and that there had been no permanent buildings, only palmetto huts. Sprague, on his visit in 1839, referred to the spring and the fort: "After wandering about Fort Mellon and seeing all there was to be seen, we crossed the lake to a spot once occupied as a fort. Here we found a most remarkable spring, strongly impregnated with sulphur; it is fully one hundred and fifty feet in circumference, and as near as we could measure, twenty feet deep." This is now called Seminole Springs (third magnitude) near the skeet range on Stone Island. Heitman also refers to the fort as temporary, while Chaffer gives its latitude as 28°52' and its longitude as 81°25'.[18] Apart from a brief mention in *The St. Johns: A Parade of Diversities,* Fort Kingsbury was cited by General Taylor in 1839 when he ordered Major Ashby with two companies of dragoons "to proceed across the country from Fort Kingsbury to Fort Pierce."[19]

The name of Fort Kingsbury probably first appeared on the Mackay and Blake Map of East Florida published by order of the Senate in 1840; Mackay and Blake were topographical engineers who first drew up the map under the direction of General Taylor. The fort also appears on the Bruff map of 1846, the original of which is in the P. K. Yonge Library of Florida History (University of Florida); Sunderman has included a reproduction of this map on page 97 of Motte's *Journey into Wilderness.* In Blackman's *History of Orange County,* Fort Kingsbury is erroneously located at the northeast end of Lake George rather than Lake Monroe; however, this is a typographical error, as reference to the map of Orange County in the same volume will reveal.[20]

On June 17, 1837, three steamboats arrived at Fort Mellon with positive orders that the post should be abandoned without delay, and Harney could no longer procrastinate. The next day Harney with four hundred dragoons (who were relocated at Fort Marion) departed for St. Augustine, leaving Coacoochee and about twenty Indians in possession of Fort Mellon. Motte presumed that the Seminoles immediately assumed command. They expressed most pacific intentions provided the whites did not molest them and promised not to burn the post; they also expressed a desire to visit Harney at St. Augustine. As late as August Osceola was reported at camp near Fort Mellon, and "Coahadjo was on the banks of the lake fishing and lived in the pickets."[21] Nevertheless the buildings at Volusia and Fort Mellon were burned by the Indians during August or September. While at St. Augustine Harney was ordered to Washington for the purpose of recruiting men to fill up the companies of the Second Dragoons. From August to November Harney was at St. Augustine in command of the First Division Army of the South.[22]

I have noted the procrastination of the Seminoles during the Capitulation at Fort Mellon, as well as the precipitate action of Osceola and Coacoochee that freed the assembled Seminoles at Tampa and doomed the Armistice to failure. Beyond that, the summer shutdown of the fort gave the Indians even more time to rest and regroup. Accordingly, there was not much organized military activity from the time of the battle at Camp Monroe in February until after the reopening of Fort Mellon in November.

Chapter 5
Exploration
from Fort Mellon

We have possessed Florida sixteen years but we have, perhaps, as little knowledge of the interior of Florida as of the interior of China.

Gen. Thomas S. Jesup, April 9, 1837

An order to proceed by sunrise tomorrow in the Steam Boats Santee & McLean to the highest accessible point of Lake Harney to establish a post on its West bank.

Lt. John Pickell, November 19, 1837

General Jesup was not idle during the summer slowdown — his thoughts turned to replenishing the army with clothing and obtaining recruits to fill out the skeleton companies with new men and officers who were not interested in becoming "schoolmasters at West Point." Personally, he did long for a few weeks' visit to Kentucky, if he were not relieved from command of the army as he had requested. If another campaign were necessary, he wanted to give himself or a new commander plenty of time, for he stated that no operations should be attempted before October.[1]

Jesup had already spoken (May 8, 1837) of the need to explore the St. Johns above Fort Mellon. On August 10 he ordered Harney to reoccupy Fort Mellon, stating, "I purpose to make Fort Mellon a principal depot, and establish posts south of it on the river and southwest of it." The Fort Mellon minimum garrison, he felt, should number 160, second only to Fort Brooke at Tampa Bay with 200.[2]

Bearing on the subject of explora-
tion are the two maps recently discovered at the National Archives, one
dated November 10, 1837, the other undated. The latter was drawn by
1st Lt. Richard C. Peyton of the Second Artillery, a graduate of the
United States Military Academy; Peyton had been in Florida since at
least 1836 and was at Fort Mellon in March, April, and May of 1837, as
reported in the post returns. He was still at the fort on June 11 when
Motte met him there. Lt. William B. Davidson, who drew the
November 10 map, reported that Peyton had discovered Lake Jessup on
May 22, 1837, when he ascended the St. Johns to that lake with a
detachment of artillery from Fort Mellon. Peyton's May 22 exploration
seems to have been the product of General Jesup's May 8 resolve to
explore the St. Johns above Fort Mellon. The resultant Peyton map
(facing this page) features Lake Jessup and also shows Fort Mellon and
the river about thirty miles upstream but does not include Lake Harney.
On the northeast corner Peyton does refer to Lake Harney: "The river
here runs on unexplored by white men. There's a large lake 4 miles above
this point." Davidson corroborates this statement by saying that nothing
was known of the St. Johns beyond Lake Jessup until the tenth of
November following, when he and Lieutenant Colonel Harney proposed
a further exploration. Peyton over his own signature has written: "The
above map has been very hastily executed but it may serve to give an idea
of the River and the courses as comparatively accurate, the distances laid
down nearly so."

Another clue as to the date of this
map and why Peyton drafted it is given by John Lee Williams, whom
Peyton told that Lake Jessup had been discovered by Peyton in the spring
of 1837 and named Lake Peyton, which name Williams reproduces on
the map of Florida appended to his book. Williams' description of the
lake, which causes one to wonder whether he had a copy of Peyton's map
before him, reads:

> Seven miles above Lake Mon-
> roe, Lake Peyton joins the river on the west side, at the extremity
> of a long sharp bend. It extends to the westward fourteen miles in
> an oval form, becoming narrow toward each end; the eastern, is
> indeed scarcely half a mile wide for a considerable distance. In the
> centre, where the width is perhaps five miles there is a circular
> island with a shoal extending to some distance toward the east.
> The water of the lake is usually six feet deep, except the east end
> which is no more than three feet. The eastern part of the lake is
> bordered with cypress swamp. The western part by hammocks
> covered with cabbage palms, live oaks and other hard timbers. A
> large Indian old field lies on the south side of the lake near the end.

30

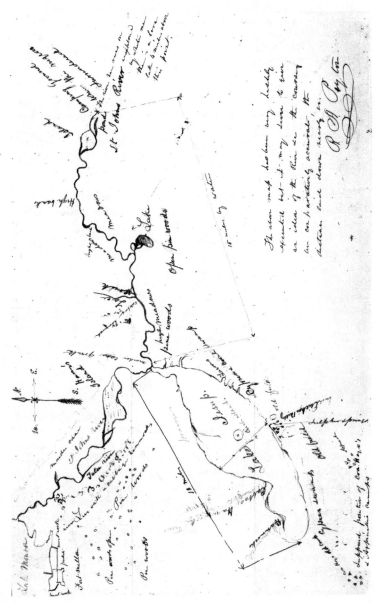

Map of Lake Jessup and the Fort Mellon
area. Drawn by Lt. Richard Peyton after
his discovery of the lake on May 22, 1837.
(National Archives)

Near it a considerable stream passes into the lake; this stream rises about a mile from the lake in several large sulphur springs. On the west side of the stream, on the lake shore is a considerable Seminole village.

Two miles below Peyton Lake, the river embraces a large island, near three miles long and one broad.

The country here, is diversified with grass savannas, swells of pine land, oak hammocks and clumps of palms; in many places near the river, the grass meadows are rich and beautiful.

Four miles from the island the river enters Lake Monroe over a sand bar on which there is little more than three feet water.[3]

Peyton's map labeled the lake with some of the same terminology that Williams uses: "circle island," "old field," "sulphurus springs," and "cypress swamps." "Old field" refers to former fields adjacent to an abandoned village. (The site of Tallahassee was called by the same name.) Opposite Circle Island (today called Bird Island) is shown Yuchi Billy's camp — later in the year at Fort Peyton, near St. Augustine, Peyton helped to capture Yuchi Billy (Billy Hicks), the son of John Hicks. Today, a third magnitude spring called Clifton Springs still flows on the south shore at Hiley's Fish Camp.[4] The large island, "near three miles long and one broad," is marked by Peyton two miles below the lake as "Harney's island." It should be aso noted that Peyton spelled "Jesup" correctly (with one s), even though it probably hurt him not to be able to use his own name, which might not have had the approval of his superiors.

Perhaps if Francis Harper had been able to make a close comparison between Williams' description and Peyton's map, he would not have questioned Williams' statement that Peyton had discovered Lake Jessup in 1837. On the other hand, Harper is right to say that the lake must have remained virtually unknown for many years after John Bartram had discovered it in 1766.[5] The rediscovery of the lake by Peyton seventy-one years later as now documented by Peyton's map does constitute an interval of "many years."

It should be pointed out that though Peyton's name apparently did not long remain attached to the lake, he did have the fort he commanded named after him. Fort Peyton was seven miles south of St. Augustine near Moultrie Creek and was formed by four log houses built in a square: two were troop barracks, one was for officers, and the fourth was used as a hospital and commissary store.[6]

As is evident from the Jesup quotation at the beginning of this chapter, little was known about the Florida interior in 1837. Writing that same year, John Lee Williams observed that half the territory of Florida had not been surveyed and that only a small portion was inhabited. He also pointed out the anomaly of exploring the South Seas but not Florida. Jesup, commenting on another aspect of the situation, made this unique observation: "We exhibit, in our present contest, the first instance, perhaps, since the commencement of authentic history, of a nation employing an army to explore a country, (for we can do little more than explore it,) or attempting to remove a band of savages from one unexplored wilderness to another."[7]

Practical necessity obliged Jesup to be guided by his own admonition that no action should be undertaken before October. Actually it was not until November that substantial exploration began, which introduces Davidson's Fort Mellon map of November 10, 1837 (see pp. 36-37); the rather extensive notations appearing on it over his signature serve as a preface to the map and illustrate the process of "employing an army to explore a country":

A rough draft of the length depth and courses of the river St. Johns E. F. [East Florida] from the head of Lake Monroe to the head of Lake Harney. The distance between these two points is laid down at 40 miles; and although estimated by the run of the Steam Boat per hour, is believed to be very near the true distance. No obstructions were met with in any part of the river, which generally at present affords an average depth of about 8 feet, until we reached the head of Lake Harney and here further progress in the Steam Boat was arrested by a bar which gives only 3½ feet water. Over the bar, the river was found to be of the usual depth, 8 feet, and appears to wind same for many miles through extensive low savannas and rushes in an easterly direction. The country here becomes very open.

The above information is the result of an expedition made up the St. Johns on the 10th Nov 1837, by the Commanding officer of Fort Mellon, Lieut Col Harney, on the steamer Santee. Capt. Poinsett having a company of artillery on board — No indians were seen, but fresh signs of them, such as newly felled trees, little rafts etc. were frequently discovered along the banks. A landing was made with 20 men at the indian town on the east shore of Lake Harney, where 20 or 30 indian huts are situated in a place strikingly beautiful cooking utensils and other indian furniture were found in and about the huts — no doubt was entertained from various signs that indians were there the day before — Six or seven acres had been cultivated in corn and pumkins. From the head of Lake Harney easterly, the eye stretches over a great extent of low savannas and appearances indicated the presence of another large lake not far distant or the beginning of the everglades.

WBD[8]

As noted earlier this map resulted from the November 10 expedition made up the St. Johns by Lieutenant Colonel Harney and Lieutenant Davidson on the steamboat *Santee*. The two officers proposed to ascertain whether the river afforded any additional facilities for the transportation of supplies and the establishment of depots. They were supported by Company F of the Third Artillery from Fort Mellon. Davidson stated further in his commentary that nothing had been known of the St. Johns beyond Lake Jessup until the November 10 expedition to Lake Harney. It must have been a thrilling moment for Colonel Harney to stand on the deck of the *Santee* and see for the first time the lake that was to bear his name.

In addition to his November 10 map, Davidson left his imprint on another map; on the right-hand and bottom margins of army engineer map L247-2 (depicting the theater of military operations in Florida during 1835-37), he, in a most minuscule script, penned in an approximately one-thousand-word commentary (transcribed as Appendix C). Together with Davidson's notes on his November 10 map of Fort Mellon, this commentary represents the fourth of the Fort Mellon original accounts, all written in 1837. Davidson's habit of putting important data on the margins of maps seems to stem from a notation by Major General Macomb, U.S. commander in chief (itself written on the margin of map L247-1), that specifically invited officers to amend maps with any information they might obtain as to the topography and return them to the adjutant general, so that a correct map of the theater of war in Florida might be drawn for the use of the War Department.

The Library of Congress possesses two manuscripts of Lt. John Pickell. One very short one is entitled "Notes of the Seminole Expedition" and is dated 1836; the other manuscript, of over seventy-seven hundred words, the longest of the five Fort Mellon accounts, is called "Brief Notes of the campaign against the Seminole Indians in Florida, in 1837" (transcribed as Appendix B). These were acquired by the Library of Congress in 1919 from C. Russell Pickell of Washington, D.C. (The 1836 manuscript was a gift; the 1837 one was purchased.) Frank L. White, Jr., has edited both accounts in the *Florida Historical Quarterly* under the title "The Journals of Lieutenant John Pickell 1836-1837." However, neither the original titles nor the one given by White convey the actual content of the manuscripts—the 1837 account could easily bear the title "Fort Mellon Daily Notes from November 8 to December 16, 1837, by Lt. John Pickell." Pickell himself, in making oblique reference to his record-keeping effort, spoke of it on one occasion as "these daily notes."

Lieutenant Pickell arrived at Fort Mellon on November 17, 1837, after a 10½-hour steamboat ride from Volusia. On his way he noted the various water birds and alligators as well as "Silver Springs," the present first magnitude Silver Glen Spring. He also remarked on the serpentine river that in a short distance could turn almost every point of the compass. The day after his arrival the troops of the Third and Fourth regiments of artillery landed and encamped a little distance from the bank of Lake Monroe on a beautiful and gentle slope.

From November 20 to 28 Pickell's entries are devoted primarily to his participation in Lieutenant Colonel Bankhead's expedition to establish a post at the highest accessible point on Lake Harney's west bank by use of the steamboats *Santee* and *McLean.* The establishment of this post, which was to become Fort Lane, was part of General Jesup's 1837 fall military campaign. From Pickell's account we learn that the expedition, comprising Companies B, F, and H of Bankhead's Third Artillery, struck its tents at sunrise on November 20 and left the Fort Mellon wharf on the two steamboats at 7:30 A.M.; the party included Pickell as adjutant, Dr. Maffit, Lieutenant Davidson, and six other lieutenants, one of them the Christopher Tompkins who received Vinton's oil portrait of Osceola. The expedition was supplied "with one six pounder and 100 rounds of ammunition, and the whole command with 100 musket ball and buckshot cartridges each and fifteen signal rockets." Exploration continued until November 28.

Davidson was an important member of the party. He considered the western shore of Lake Harney near its head (where Fort Lane was to be located) as very suitable for a depot. On the other hand, Pickell and the other officers were not of the same opinion, for they recommended a kind of floating barge depot at the head of Lake Harney or farther up the river. According to Davidson, the Fort Lane ultimate site was considered by Colonel Bankhead as to near Fort Mellon. But Jesup seems to have been more impressed by the sheet of notes that Davidson submitted outlining his position. Davidson noted Jesup's satisfaction with the move, the general having stated that "Major Dearborn was sent forward with a detachment and supplies in barges, to establish a depot at the head of Lake Harney." And Davidson felt that Dearborn had established a good post.[9]

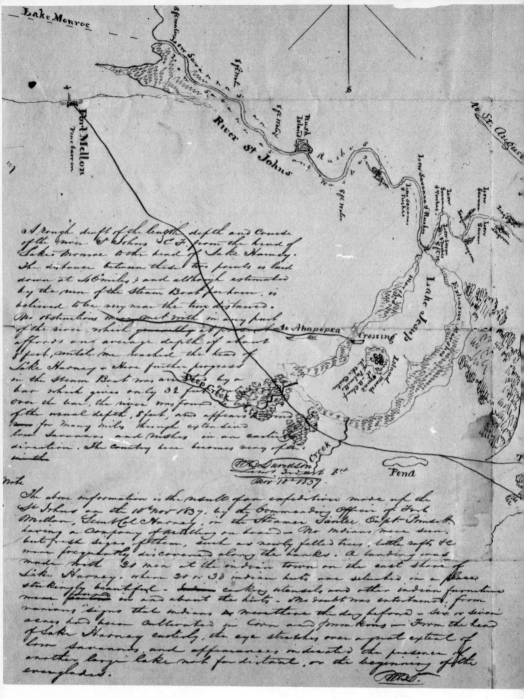

Map of Lake Harney and the Fort Mellon
area. Drawn by Lt. William Davidson after
the discovery of the lake by the Harney
expedition on November 10, 1837.
(National Archives)

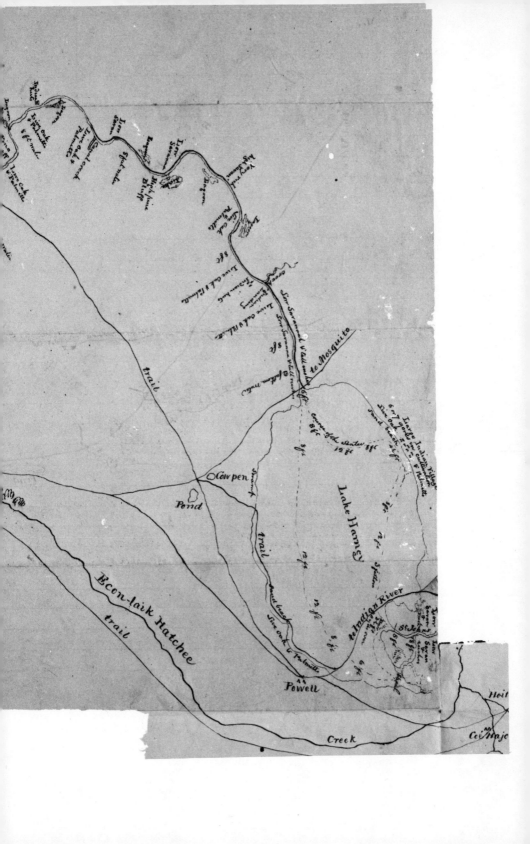

Davidson must have served as cartographer under Harney, as Pickell in his journal entry of November 22 writes that he has added his notes and sketches to those of Lieutenant Davidson. Since the Davidson expedition is dated November 10, Pickell cannot have been present when it set out. After Pickell's arrival the emphasis was on locating a depot on Lake Harney and finding the head of the river; on the other hand, Davidson indicates that his initial project was to draft the length, depth, and courses of the St. Johns from the head of Lake Monroe to the head of Lake Harney.

The descriptions and observations of Pickell and Davidson sound so alike one might think they were writing about the same expedition. Both men encountered trouble over the bar at the head of Lake Harney; both landed parties of twenty at recently vacated Indian villages where utensils, huts, corn, and pumpkins were found. Davidson notes the landing on the eastern shore, and his map indicates a "large Indian village, six or seven acres in cultivation" near present-day Stone Island (Lake Harney); however, the larger of two Indian encampments observed by Pickell was at the "upper crossing" about twenty-five miles from the lake. Pickell says that he and Davidson landed twice on the west shore of Lake Harney, looking in vain for a suitable military post location.

Reading from the Davidson commentary on army engineer map L247-2 we find the mapmaker and the journalist reporting another identical episode for November 24 (the second expedition, in which they both took part). Pickell in his entry on that day had referred to the "upper crossing." Both men relate that the steamboat *John McLean* had been sent from Fort Mellon with dispatches from General Eustis and Colonel Bankhead directing the steamboats to run up to the head of Lake Harney for the purpose of sending two barges to an upper crossing twenty to twenty-five miles above the lake. To assist in this Eustis had sent along as guide a black named Ben, who knew of the crossing and who was a slave of the Seminole chief Micanopy. Exploration proved Ben's information to be correct, and the trail was found where the Indians frequently crossed the St. Johns. Lieutenants Ross and Pickell each had charge of a barge and were accompanied by Lieutenant Tompkins with thirty men and Ben; however, the trail, which ran by where Fort Christmas was built about a month later, was found to be impracticable for transporting supplies from the river over the savannas to solid terrain.[10]

Pickell, after having given to Lieutenant Davidson the notes and sketches he had made of the upper river, states (November 22) that "we were enabled after my return to make a correct map of the river which we presented to Col. Bankhead."

This, however, could not be the Davidson map of November 10 because of the date discrepancy and because that map extends only to the head of Lake Harney. Pickell's account of exploration goes beyond the area covered by Davidson's map and notations. The lake that Pickell proudly announced as being named after him and that he erroneously identifies (November 22) as the head of the river appears to be somewhere near the southern end of the present Puzzle Lake, whose name is suggested by the *terra incognita* description Pickell used for the area. Without a doubt this is not the origin of the name Puzzle Lake; but a puzzle it did present to Pickell, who because he did not continue thought and perhaps hoped he had found the headwaters. He was certainly wrong in thinking that the Indians had not penetrated farther. He was even wrong in thinking the same of white men. In fact the early Philadelphia naturalists John and William Bartram had explored the St. Johns in 1766; they thought that they had found the headwaters at about the same longitude as Pickell declared but a little to the east, at Salt Lake.

Cabell and Hanna contend that the Bartrams (and of course Pickell) were fifty miles short. They further point out that in 1822 the naturalist John Eatton LeConte charted the course of the St. Johns for the government. LeConte states that beyond the upper course of the river a marsh extends "as far as the eye can reach . . . with as level and uninterrupted horizon as the sea itself . . . constantly under water, and therefore may be considered as one great spring . . . from which water is slowly but continually oozing out." Today we know this as the St. Johns Marsh that begins in Brevard County and extends through Indian River County down into St. Lucie County almost as far south as Fort Pierce. Cabell and Hanna point out that the waters of the marsh "are derived from the copious rainfall of South Florida; and that part of the rainfall which does not seep into the northward flowing St. Johns either drains southeast, so as to supply the St. Lucie River, or else goes southward into Lake Okeechobee and the Everglades."[11]

What we now term the St. Johns Marsh the 1837 writers called savannas. However, Davidson and Pickell distinguish everglades and savannas somewhat indifferently: to Davidson the savannas seemed to presage the beginning of the everglades, but Pickell (November 22) described the everglades as extensive savannas. John Lee Williams mentions that the elder Bartram and Colonel Gadsden had traversed an area "near the head savannas of the St. Johns river."[12]

We can appreciate that what Pickell saw looked like everglades, and his difficulty is understandable in that people even today underestimate the size of Florida. Since Pickell was an 1822 graduate of West Point, it seems doubtful he could have known of LeConte's charting of the St. Johns that same year. Nor was Pickell alone, for Davidson too imagined a possible "beginning of the everglades" just beyond Lake Harney. Pickell does admit that "towards the South the river is interminable"; besides, not everyone has a lake named after him, and we can understand his being carried away – he was in the company of Jesup, Harney, and Secretary of War Poinsett. For it was the Second Seminole War, requiring the army "to explore a country," that brought about the American rediscovery of lakes Jessup and Harney and gave rise to their present names.

As a result of exploring the upper St. Johns in 1837 Jesup was able to report the practicability of ascending the river to Fort Taylor (Lake Winder, Brevard County); however, this was not to be accomplished by steamboat navigation, the extent of which Jesup stated was limited to thirty-five miles above Fort Mellon. For exploring the St. Johns to the farthest point of boat navigation Jesup gave credit to Lieutenant Searle and Colonel Harney, each of whom achieved this feat in a boat propelled by poles and oars. Colonel Harney later repeated this strenuous ordeal with several barges loaded with forage in time for General Jesup's departure from Fort Taylor to what became the battle of the Loxahatchee.[13]

Chapter 6
The Cherokee Deputation

It is not intended that this mission shall delay ... the military
operations against the Seminoles; and ... you may delay sending
the Cherokee chiefs to them till you shall have struck a blow.
J. R. Poinsett, October 30, 1837

The last few entries in Pickell's journal take up a new subject: his colorful
and informative account of the Cherokee Deputation or "delegation," as
he always referred to it. After the failure of General Jesup's Capitulation,
other means to end the war were sought by the Martin Van Buren
administration. Accordingly, John H. Sherburne, a private agent of
Secretary of War Poinsett, proposed mediation by the Cherokee Indians,
themselves involved with the government in a similar emigration problem.[1]

    The Cherokee nation and other
southern Indian tribes had made considerable advances and had established representative governments patterned on those of the states. The
principal chief of the Cherokee nation was John Ross, whose father was a
Scot and Indian trader and whose mother was a Cherokee. Well educated, he had originated the written constitution of the Cherokee
nation; to him also is attributed the advances his people had made.[2] (The
later story of John Ross's efforts to keep the Cherokee nation neutral in
the Civil War is one of the main threads running through the plot of
Frank Slaughter's 1975 novel *The Stonewall Brigade.*)

    In Washington, where he spent
much of his time in the interests of his people, Ross was moved by the
greater sufferings of the Seminoles and volunteered the mediation services of his nation. After his offer had been sanctioned by the secretary of
war, Ross appointed five of his principal chiefs, one to act as interpreter.
This deputation, as they termed it, was composed of Tekaske (Hair
Conrad), the nominal head; Taskeketchee (Jesse Bushyhead); Anas-
taqua (Thomas Woodward); Oosaheta (Richard Fields); and
Telakaquala (Polecat), the interpreter. Oosaheta kept records and reported to Ross; Taskeketchee was a Baptist minister who later served as
chief justice of the Cherokee nation in Oklahoma.[3]

    The full deputation and Sher-
burne arrived at St. Augustine on November 10, 1837, having visited
General Jesup the day before at his Picolata headquarters. Ross did not

accompany his appointees to Florida, but he gave them a written appeal to be read "To the Chief, Head Men and Warriors of the Seminoles of Florida" and particularly to "Mickenopah [Micanopy], Osceola, and Alligator." It was dated at Washington, October 18, 1837, three days before the seizure of Osceola.

The captive audience of prisoner chiefs at St. Augustine included Osceola, Coa Hadjo, and Coacoochee, the latter of Camp Monroe battle fame. After the peace pipe had been smoked, the Seminoles sanctioned the Cherokee mission to the warriors in the forests, though Coacoochee warned them it would be dangerous to try to convince the other chiefs to move to the West. Osceola, who spoke briefly, said he was tired of fighting and too ill to say more. He had contracted the same fever that proved fatal to so many soldiers.[4]

After this meeting, the chiefs at Fort Marion (since 1942 renamed Castillo de San Marcos, the original Spanish designation of the St. Augustine fort) sent out messages (November 14) to the active chiefs advising them to come in. The Seminole messengers were expected to report at Fort Mellon on November 24, when the deputation arrived; however, they were one day late. Characteristic of Jesup's uncooperative attitude toward the Cherokees was his failure to arrive until November 26.[5]

At this time Pickell was exploring the upper St. Johns as far as "the main crossing" about fifty miles south of Fort Mellon and was thus unable to record the arrival of the Cherokees. Upon his return (November 26) he reported that Micanopy had indicated there would be a meeting with the Cherokees "at Powells creek about 60 miles from Fort Mellon" and noted that a "talk" had been held between some of the chiefs and warriors, the result of the first contact made by the Seminole messengers. Pickell further observed as a good omen the Seminoles' failure to challenge the army exploring party on coming down the river from the upper crossing. He was thus "inclined to the opinion that the last rifle had been fired."

Through the messengers, Micanopy indicated that he felt he could persuade many of his people to surrender, but he asked for a conference with the Cherokee Deputation. To this request General Jesup consented after several ambiguous discussions with the deputation, who were pressured to modify some parts of the presentation that the general considered objectionable. But Jesup did not make it easy for the Cherokees. They pointed out that they were allowed only six days' round trip to perform their peace errand and that only a day and a half remained of the four days' time schedule set by Micanopy; moreover, they would have to ride fifty miles from Fort Mellon through almost impenetrable terrain.[6]

42

Pickell's entry of Tuesday November 28, the day of the Cherokees' first mission from Fort Mellon, carries on the story very colorfully and effectively:

> The arrangements with the delegation of the Cherokee chiefs having been made for their departure, they left the Camp at 2 o'clk, P.M. to meet the Seminole Chiefs in council at Powell creek said to be 50 miles distant in a S.Westerly direction. After going through the ceremony of shaking hands they mounted their horses and rode slowly through the camp. The delegation 5 in number headed by the celebrated Seminole Chief Co-a-hadjo, attired in the rich costume of his nation, presented an imposing spectacle and left us with our best wishes for their success in their errand of peace. God grant they may succeed and prevail upon the hostile chiefs to come in, and yield without further bloodshed to the necessity which they cannot by any means obviate. The opinion of the officers is that the delegation will be successful. It is expected to return by Saturday next. That day so important to our future operations, is awaited with the most patient anxiety.

The tenor of the deputation's report to John Ross, as well as Jesup's own words and actions, strongly suggests that the general did not share Pickell's hopes for the success of the peace mission. Jesup was known as a crusty old Indian fighter; moreover, Poinsett had recommended that Jesup make some move against the Seminoles before the deputation reached the Florida Indians and had warned the general to see that the Cherokees did not exceed their authority. (See Poinsett's remark at the beginning of this chapter.) On the other hand, Ross was skeptical of government promises to reward him with more lenient terms in his own negotiations. In this atmosphere of mutual mistrust success was unlikely.[7]

On two points Pickell and the deputation's report differ. The former gives the time of departure as 2:00 P.M.; on the twenty-eighth the latter put it at "about" 10:00 A.M. Secondly, Pickell gives the council meeting place as "Powells Creek," while the Cherokee mention "Totalousy Hatchy, a small branch of the St. Johns." Since the latter name translates into "Chicken Creek," Pickell may have misheard "Fowl" as "Powell." ("Fowl Town" in Decatur County, Georgia, derived from this same Indian name.) Furthermore, Motte actually gives the name of the meeting place as "Fowl Town," as does the Savannah *Georgian*, except that they refer to it as "Fowl Towns."

This area is now in the 28,000-acre tract that for the last fifty years has been called Tosohatchee Game Preserve and that the Florida Department of Natural Resources has purchased under the endangered lands program. The Indian name was

43

shortened from Tootoosahatchee to Tosohatchee when the game club was incorporated, according to Mr. William Beardall, one of its principals and former mayor of Orlando.[8]

At midday on November 29 the Cherokee Deputation led by Coa Hadjo, who was released from captivity to act as a guide to the five mediators in their errand of peace, found no one at the appointed place. The Cherokee report to John Ross explained that the Seminoles had discovered a party of troops landing at Lake Harney and had concluded that the Cherokees intended to deceive them. This report confirms Pickell's November 26 observation that there had been "afforded hundreds of opportunities" for his party to have been seen by the Seminoles; but instead of the hostility he anticipated, mistrust was registered. In his entry of December 3, Pickell also confirms that the command under Colonel Bankhead up the river had been seen by the Indians.[9]

The next morning Coa Hadjo, after some scouting, led the deputation from Tootoosahatchee twelve miles farther south to Chickasaw Hatchee (present-day Taylor Creek), where Micanopy and his chiefs were assembled. (Both rivers flow into the St. Johns just north of Lake Poinsett.)[10] There the Cherokee peace pipe was produced and laid on the ground between the deputation and Micanopy. After a few brief introductory remarks by Tekaske, the appeal of John Ross was read by Oosaheta and interpreted by Taskeketchee. It began, "I address you in the name of the Cherokee nation, as its principal chief, and with the feeling of a brother hold out to you the hand of friendship," and continued:

> I know that a brave people when driven to a state of desperation, would sooner die under the strong arm of power, than to shrink and die the death of the coward. But I will speak to you as a friend, and with the voice of reason advise you, as a small but a brave people, to act the part of a noble race, and at once throw yourselves upon the magnanimity and justice of the American people.[11]

The deputation also pointed out that the Seminoles and the Cherokees were then the only southern Indians east of the Mississippi River and that as brother Indians they should settle their difficulties together with the United States in a peaceable and friendly way.[12]

This first effort produced results, and on December 2 the deputation set out for Fort Mellon accompanied by Micanopy, Yaholoochee, and eleven subchiefs including Tuskegee and Nocose Yohola, plus some warriors, twenty-five or thirty in all. Late in the evening of December 3 they "reached the encampment of the

Army before Fort Mellon with the white scarf of peace rippling over our heads, and after partaking of some refreshments, we called on Genl. Jesup."[13] Their purpose in coming was not to surrender but to negotiate with General Jesup.

Pickell's entry in his journal of December 3 confirms the return of the delegation that day and notes the appearance of Micanopy, Yaholoochee, and Coa Hadjo under a white flag; it adds that Arpeika, who was not well enough to ride the fifty to sixty miles (he was upwards of seventy years old), sent his nephew to say that if General Jesup would treat his nephew well and send one of the Cherokees to him, he would come in with all his warriors (about four hundred). Both Arpeika and Coa Hadjo signed the Treaty of Payne's Landing. Coa Hadjo, who was chief of the Seminoles east of Lake Tohopekaliga (present Osceola County), was one of the delegation sent west of the Mississippi to examine the country in accordance with the terms of the treaty. Arpeika at one time was a Mikasuki chief around Silver Springs; later in the war he occupied the country near the mouth of the Kissimmee River on the eastern border of Lake Okeechobee.[14]

The Cherokees described Jesup's reception as cold and almost repulsive, with not a sign of approbation. Jesup seemed to be using them for a source of military intelligence, judging by the questions he asked.[15] Pickell fills in some points that the Cherokee report to John Ross does not cover — he presents a very graphic picture in his entry of December 5, when at noon the "talk" was held with the chief and warriors in the area in front of General Jesup's tent. Seated on benches were Micanopy in the middle, Yaholoochee and Coa Hadjo on his left, and Tuskegee and one other on his right. Micanopy pledged that if Indian runners were allowed to go out, Arpeika, Ote Emathla, and the other chiefs would come in and surrender their arms. As a guarantee of this promise Jesup required that the women and children of the Indians nearest the camp as well as those of the captives in St. Augustine be brought in at once. The chiefs then selected the runners to be equipped with horses and provisions for the round trip to the chiefs who had not come in. The runner to Arpeika was directed to return in seven days, the runner to Ote Emathla in ten days.

Thus it would seem that a double effort was being made — by the Seminole chiefs at Fort Mellon as well as by the Cherokees — to contact the reluctant and more militant chiefs. In his entry of December 4 Pickell notes the report that a Cherokee would leave that night to carry the "talk" to Arpeika. As related in the Cherokee report, Taskeketchee and an interpreter left December 6 to assure Arpeika of General Jesup's strong desire to make peace. But the escape of Coacoochee changed Arpeika's mind. Coacoochee was quoted as saying that he never knew before that women and children had to go and make peace and that it was the duty of the chiefs and men to do such business. He also suspected the Cherokees of "acting the double part of deceivers."[16] On November 29, Coacoochee had escaped from his incarceration at Fort Marion, St. Augustine, by forcing himself through a narrow opening in the masonry wall. Pickell had been apprehensive (December 2) that the first Cherokee mission from Fort Mellon on November 28 would be affected by Coacoochee's escape; however, the escape came too late to prevent Micanopy and the others from coming to Fort Mellon. On the other hand, Pickell's fears about Coacoochee reaching Arpeika were sound insofar as the second Cherokee mission was concerned, for Taskeketchee and Oosaheta were told "that Wildcat had destroyed all the plans of peace."[17] Pickell adds (December 14) that Arpeika was quoted as saying that he "was ready to give them battle whenever they came into his country."

On December 12 Pickell wrote that Taskeketchee and one of Yaholoochee's men had returned at dusk and that Taskeketchee had not been as successful as Pickell had wished; he continues:

> A-bi-a-ca [Arpeika] does not appear to be disposed to surrender. Jumper says he will come in but is lame and cannot walk fast. Genl. Jessup will send a horse to him. After Bushy-head's return to camp a "talk" was held in front of Genl. Jessup's tent, at which Micanopy, Cloud and several of the sub-chiefs attended. The General gave the Chiefs to understand that no more time can be lost and that Co-a-coo-chee, Tus-ke-nug-gee, Miceo and one other must be surrendered at once, and that he would not listen to terms of peace unless they were brought in. The return of Bushy head produced a considerable excitement in camp. We had been expecting him since morning. His return would bring us intelligence of an important character and which would determine the character of our operations. If the Indians would come in with him, no more blood would be shed. If they refused and persisted in their hostilities they would be met as enemies in war and be dealt with accordingly.

Although pessimistic, Taskeketchee made a third and final attempt after 7:00 P.M. on December 12.[18] Pickell (December 12) explains:

> Bushy-head and Mr. Fields two of the delegation are determined if the hostiles can be prevailed upon to yield, to leave no efforts untried. They will leave to night and expect to be with Abiaca by 11 o'clk tomorrow morning. Bushy head said the last words he spoke to A-bi-a-ca when he found he was not willing to yield to his persuasions was ["] Well, Abiaca the consequences will be upon your head. The blood that

46

will be shed you will be answerable for, if you will not regard my advice, farewell."

Taskeketchee's final attempt was prompted by an encouraging message from some of the Seminole chiefs brought by the young Seminole who had accompanied him and his interpreter back to Fort Mellon after the second mission. Taskeketchee, Oosaheta, and their interpreter set out immediately with the young Seminole accompanying them again; the message, however, turned out to be what Pickell termed in the last entry of his commentary "a deep *ruse de guerre*," for the youth admitted that the chiefs and their people had gone south as soon as Taskeketchee had left and that he had been instructed by the chiefs to make up a story to deceive the Cherokees. The Seminoles, he said, had determined to "fight and die on the land that the Great Spirit had given them."[19]

Both Pickell and the Cherokee report note the return of Taskeketchee and Oosaheta to Fort Mellon on December 14. The Cherokee mediation had been a failure because Arpeika and his people had "let the words of the talk enter one ear and pass through the other like the listless winds"; yet it might have succeeded but for the escape of Coacoochee and the harsh demands of Jesup for "an entire surrender of their arms, their wives, and their children and to conform unconditionally to the provisions of a former treaty against which they stood in open hostility."[20]

As the prospects of the Cherokee mission diminished, Pickell's initial optimism also waned. A philosophical portion of his December 4 entry reflects this:

Parleying with the Indians gives them only hopes that cannot be fulfilled. . . . Promptness. . . would have had the effect we all most earnestly desire – an unconditional surrender and consequently a termination of hostilities. The Commanding General has no doubt acted at this important crisis upon the most mature deliberation, and after weighing in his mind the consequences that might result from the several modes that presented themselves to his mind from all the lights with which he had been furnished. I must confess, that my belief in the sincerity of the Indian Chiefs who have come in with the exception of Micanopy and Co-a-hadjo is a little impaired by their apparent indifference & manner here. I hope I am mistaken.

Immediately after the Cherokees had informed Jesup of the failure of their mission, he ordered all who had come in "to be sent off instantly to St. Augustine as *prisoners of war, or rather, as captives, who had come in under a flag of peace,* by our persuasion,

47

and under the auspices of our mediator." The italics used by the deputation reflect its feelings of indignation, frustration, and remorse.[21] Pickell
in his entry of December 14 enumerates the count as including seventy-
two Indians, women, children, and blacks, plus Micanopy and Coa
Hadjo with about thirty fighting men. Twenty-four rifles were confis-
cated. At 2:00 P.M. the steamboat *Santee* left Fort Mellon for St. Augustine with the captives and a guard of twenty-one. Pickell adds that
Yaholoochee reportedly shed tears when aboard the *Santee* but opines
that since Yaholoochee had a villainous look, he was lamenting the
impossibility of escape rather than anything else. Pickell also thought
that Micanopy and the noble-looking Coa Hadjo were sincere in their
professions of peace and friendship.

           The Cherokee Deputation oc-
cupied Pickell's attention up until and including his last entry, December
16, when he noted that at 9:00 A.M. the steamboat *Camden* took the
delegation to Black Creek. In his closing remarks Pickell acts as an
apologist for the unsuccessful negotiations between the hostile Indians
and the government:

> The Indians played a deep *ruse de guerre* by the deception they
> practiced upon the delegation and upon the army. The delay it has
> caused, they have availed themselves of, no doubt either to move
> farther south and to a country still more inaccessible to the Army,
> or otherwise strengthened themselves, while we were quietly
> awaiting the fulfillment of their promises & pledges at the day that
> was designated at the "talk."
>
>   Every disposition has been
> manifested on the part of the Commanding General to promote
> the object of the Delegation and to induce the Indians to surrender,
> without further resistance and which would result unavoidably to
> the serious injury of Indians as a people & as a nation. This we are
> all exceedingly desirous to avoid and had hoped the Cherokee
> Delegation who have no doubt very honestly and sincerely used
> every exertion to prevail upon A-bi-a-ca (Sam Jones) the most
> important & influential Chief of the hostiles to yield to their
> wishes and prevent the farther affusion of blood, and perhaps their
> extermination as a people. The consequences of their continued
> resistance has been represented to them. They are aware of what
> will follow. The Commanding General distinctly informed the
> runners when they went out, that if one drop of blood was shed by
> any one of them, the captives would be executed, & that it would
> most assuredly be carried into effect.... in justice to the Command-
> ing General it is due to state that every indulgence every persuasion
> every means consistent with the policy of the government has been
> regarded and used to terminate, without the alternative of arms,

this protracted war by the mediation of the Cherokee Delegation to which the War Department has given much importance by its sanction and acceptance.

The Cherokees were naturally anxious to vindicate themselves to the chiefs at St. Augustine, and they promised to get the captives released. On Christmas the deputation reached Charleston, where Colonel Sherburne persuaded it to accompany him to Washington for the purpose of "sustaining him."[22]

In Washington John Ross was unable to get any satisfaction — even the remuneration that was due the deputation was disputed by Poinsett over portal-to-portal considerations.[23] The deputation rightly felt that it could be suspected of entrapping the Seminoles, since it had been instrumental in persuading Micanopy and the others to go to Fort Mellon and had unwittingly furthered Jesup's dragnet program of capturing and removing Seminoles from Florida. The Cherokees were eventually able to negotiate a treaty for themselves, which entertained their agreement to move to Oklahoma, but they failed to persuade their Florida brothers, primarily because the most influential Seminole chiefs would not agree to removal. What the Cherokees had to face is well summarized by Jesup's comment: "That talk contained, as I thought, propositions at variance with my instructions. It held out to the Seminoles the promise of a treaty; but I was required to enforce the provisions of an *existing treaty*, not to make a *new treaty*."[24] Neither the mediation of the Cherokees nor that of any other agency could have been expected to prevail over the unyielding positions set by the two protagonists of the Second Seminole War.

Jesup seems to have hoped for evidence to justify the failure of the Cherokee mediation. On January 2, 1838, when writing from "Headquarters Army of the South, Fort Christmas," he took great satisfaction in reporting to Poinsett the following: One of the Seminole chiefs, Ote Emathla (Jumper) had indicated to Col. Zachary Taylor about the time of the battle of Okeechobee that the Cherokees had told the Seminoles the latter could remain in Florida upon "certain conditions." Jesup concluded "we now have the evidence of Jumper as to the bad faith of the Cherokees."[25] He even imagined that with the money paid to the Cherokees for leaving their Alabama and Georgia lands John Ross would have the means to rally the Indians west of the Mississippi, as well as the blacks within the southern states and the territory of Florida, against the United States. This rather uncharacteristic reaction of Jesup seems unjustified, since there is no evidence that John Ross ever entertained such ambitions — on the contrary, even before the Second Seminole War ended John Ross was to lead his people in the pathetic, bitter, and debilitating government-enforced emigration to-ward the setting sun beyond the Mississippi—a journey that the Cherokees called "The Trail of Tears" and that Gloria Jahoda used as the title of one of her recent books.

It is interesting and of historical significance to note how Lieutenant Pickell's commentary, focused on Fort Mellon, so closely corroborates the Cherokee Deputation's report while adding other colorful details and comments.

Chapter 7
Steamboats at Fort Mellon

> We cannot calculate with certainty on steamboat navigation more
> than thirty five miles above [Fort Mellon], unless boats of less draft
> can be obtained.
>
> Gen. Thomas S. Jesup, November 29, 1837

Steamboats played a significant role in the life of Fort Mellon: in the
battle of Camp Monroe, in providing transportation for Indian removal,
in exploring the St. Johns, and in connection with military logistics
throughout the year. Jesup's order 36 (January 1837) specified "Steam
Boats of sufficiently light draft to ascend the St. Johns into Lake Monroe,
and of sufficient power to tow the barges on that river."[1] Pickell names
seven of these steamboats that ascended the St. Johns, "the grand artery
of the country":[2] the *Camden,* the *Charleston,* the *Cincinnati,* the *Forrester,* the *James Adams,* the *McLean,* and the *Santee.* Colonel Fanning adds
two others, the *John Stoney,* which arrived just after the battle on
February 9, and the *Essayons,* whose captain (along with the *Santee's*) he
praised after the battle. The role of these nine steamboats has been an
unappreciated facet of the Fort Mellon story. Only thirty years had passed
since Fulton's *Clermont;* only thirteen had passed since the Supreme
Court had ruled all waters of the country free and not subject to state
monopolies granted privileged steamboat owners. Moreover, the Fort
Mellon boats preceded by thirty-five years the golden age of steamboating on the St. Johns in the heyday of the Brock, DeBary, and Clyde lines,
though in the 1845-55 years limited and sometimes sporadic service on
the upper St. Johns was provided by the *Sarah Spaulding,* the *Hancock,*
the *Thorn,* the *Welaka,* and the *Darlington.*
                                      Although so much steamboat ac-
tivity at Fort Mellon may seem surprising, it should be noted that the St.
Johns was quite navigable apart from its mouth and the bars at the
southern ends of lakes George, Monroe, and Harney. Steamboats solved
many logistical and transportation problems of the Second Seminole
War and were readily available from nearby Charleston and Savannah.[3]
Jesup was not unmindful of the navigational problems: several times in
1837 he attempted to have the dredge boat working at the mouth of the
river sent upstream to remove the bars at the heads of lakes George and
Monroe so as to make the river "an avenue for the transportation of
troops and supplies near two hundred miles." He seems to have been at
least partially successful, for a correspondent of the *New York Commercial*

Advertiser reported (November 14, 1837) that while steaming up the St. Johns on the *Santee* the steamer *Camden* was met guarding a dredge boat clearing the bar at the head of Lake George.[4] This dredging activity, in which logistical planning Fort Mellon was included, is most likely one of the first such navigational improvements undertaken by the Army Corps of Engineers. Until now their information (in two letters from the Office of the Chief of Engineers, September 3, 1975, and July 1, 1976) had indicated that the first corps dredging on inland rivers did not take place until the late 1840s.

Surgeon Motte's account of his passage to Fort Mellon on the *Essayons* in June of 1837 illustrates the difficulty at this bar: the very same 169-ton *Camden*, aground, had been met by the *Essayons*, and it had been necessary to unload the troops and transfer them to the *Essayons*, which drew less water. So it seems only proper that the *Camden* should have been the boat assigned to the dredge guard duty five months later at the same spot. Similar navigational problems were related by Pickell (November 20-23), in connection with the *Santee* and the *McLean* at the bars at lakes Monroe and Harney: the *Santee* loaded needed four feet plus a few inches; the *McLean* if lightened of cargo could float across three feet eight inches but grounded at three feet six inches. The previous year Gen. Winfield Scott had found that the *Essayons* could not exit the southern end of Lake Monroe because "our boat drew more than four feet and we found only four feet on the bar." Writing later, General Scott was less than complimentary to the *Essayons* when he referred to her as "a miserable little steamer."[5]

Regarding water level, Pickell noted on November 21 that "bushes and grass along the shore showed that the water had been lately about 4 ft. higher than at present," and John Lee Williams is quoted as saying that "cholera morbus" was attributed to the rapid lowering of the water level in the lake and river. The *Niles' Weekly Register* of July 8, 1837, referred to rumors that the epidemic at Fort Mellon was Asiatic cholera but discounted them because the sudden and continued falling of the lake exposing putrid and partially decomposed vegetation to temperatures of eighty-five to ninety degrees revealed that the disease was of purely local origin. The paper further explained that after a heavy rain, all traces of the disease disappeared. Jesup, when complaining about the loss of fifteen important days during the negotiations of the Cherokee Deputation, pointed out that "the water in the St. Johns has fallen so low as to compel me to use the boats propelled by oars and poles, to transport supplies to the depots which I found it necessary to establish further south on that river."[6] The levels of the St. Johns system fluctuate as much today as they did then.

Steamboat at Volusia. Greene &
McGowran lithograph, 1837. (John Lee
Williams, The Territory of Florida, *facing*
page 56)

The Fort Mellon steamboats, tie-
ing in with the steam packets from Washington to Charleston (South
Carolina), put Washington only five days from the war zone. Leaving
Washington on Friday, the packet arrived at Charleston the following
Monday; a connecting steamer ran up the St. Johns and returned to meet
the Charleston packet leaving on Friday and reaching Washington on
Monday, ten days after the original departure.[7] How best to implement
this important service – whether to contract or purchase steamboats –
was a consideration. Jesup felt that if the war lasted beyond 1837 it would
be less costly to purchase all steamboats required but that if a single
campaign should end the war it would be less expensive to hire them,
considering the loss to be expected on their resale after only one year. He
also estimated that four steamboats would be required on the St. Johns

below Fort Mellon and two of lighter draft above. Although three steamboats that the War Department had purchased in 1836 operated in Gulf coast areas, Jesup considered that on the Gulf coast between Tampa and New Orleans sailing vessels would be better employed.[8]

The decision was to charter steamboats, as is clear from a resolution of the Senate at the close of 1837 authorizing an audit of steam vessels employed in the service of the United States in the Second Seminole War. From time and rate schedules it can be seen that the 170-ton *Santee's* role in the battle at Camp Monroe was part of a ten-month stint (November 13, 1836-September 13, 1837) at $3900 per month. Although the Treasury Department's auditor shows no figures after September 13, 1837, it is likely that in November of 1837 the *Santee* was exploring the upper St. Johns at the same $3900 monthly rate, with the 133-ton *McLean* at $4000 as before. (The *Santee's* charges had escalated from an original monthly charge of $2200 in 1836.) The 155-ton *John Stoney*, reported at Fort Mellon the day after the battle, had been hired for $3000 per month on a one-year engagement (September 8, 1836-September 8, 1837).

Other steamboats were the Savannah-built, 148-ton *Forrester* at $3500, the 211-ton *Cincinnati* at $2000 to $4000, and the 205-ton *Charleston*, most expensive at $3750 to $4400. The *Santee, Cincinnati, Charleston*, and the *Camden*, all sidewheelers, were built in Charleston between 1835 and 1837; the *John Stoney* was built in New York in 1830.[9]

Because of her close association with the Fort Mellon area in 1837, the *Santee* might well be considered the "Fort Mellon boat" and thus should be of special interest to Sanford. We do not know her dimensions, though Pickell's observations show that she drew slightly over four feet. Comparable vessels of equal tonnage were about one hundred and twenty feet long, twenty feet wide, and seven feet deep.[10] Representations, verbal or pictorial, of these early steamboats are rare, but a December 1836 newspaper advertisement for the sale of the somewhat smaller *Etiwan* furnishes particulars that could also be characteristic of the *Santee*. The *Etiwan*, with a coppered and copper-fastened hull, had heavy copper boilers and a ninety-horsepower, low-pressure engine manufactured by Fawsett, Preston and Company of Liverpool. Her equipment also included a copper-riveted leather fire hose with a copper discharge pipe, and her five-man crew seem to have been slaves. The *Santee's* captain was a certain Brooks (identified as Horace Brooks by Mahon in his index to Sprague's *Florida War*), whom Fanning praised after the battle of Camp Monroe and who may have been the same Captain Brooks of the *General Clinch* in 1843 and of the *Calhoun* in 1853, as reported in St. Augustine and Savannah papers.[11]

In January of 1836 the *Santee* had been chartered by a committee of concerned Charleston citizens to carry troops (the German Fusileers and the Hamburg Volunteers) and arms under General Eustis to St. Augustine; the two-day trip cost $200. After his reconnaissance to Fort Florida near the end of April, General Scott ordered those at Volusia with malignant bilious fever approaching yellow fever to be evacuated on the *Santee* and the *Essayons*. During the first campaign of General Call in October, the *Santee* along with the *John Stoney* and the *Charleston,* leased at $1500, $3000, and $3750 per month, respectively, and loaded with stores and with two schooners in tow, were sent to the head of Lake George. Six days before Christmas and still on charter to the army, the *Santee* helped rescue survivors from the steamboat *Dolphin,* which had blown up near the St. Johns bar at the mouth of the river.

In February of 1837 the *Santee* cannonaded herself into the history of Sanford. Being "constantly on the *qui vive*" on the way to Fort Mellon in November 1837, as a correspondent reported from Volusia, the *Santee* had bulwarks constructed all around and at its bow a six pounder "levelled and primed."[12] As a matter of fact, Jesup's ordering (January 10, 1837) the first steamboat up the river to Fort Mellon to be "so barricaded as to protect the crew from the fire of the enemy and armed with a field piece" had set a pattern, and Captain Brooks had not forgotten the effectiveness of a six pounder at Fort Mellon in February.

On June 29, 1837, the St. Augustine *Florida Herald* reported that several days prior a quarrel had taken place between the cook and the steward of the *Santee* and that in the course of the scuffle the steward had been knocked overboard and drowned.

I already have mentioned the *Santee's* role in explorations above Fort Mellon during November 1837, including the discovery of Lake Harney. Pickell reports some half-dozen arrivals and departures of the *Santee,* including his own arrival, the return to Volusia of General Jesup and staff, and the transfer of seventy-two Seminoles along with Micanopy and Coa Hadjo to St. Augustine. Pickell cites the *Camden* as carrying the departing Cherokee Deputation from Fort Mellon, but the December 30, 1837, issue of the *Niles' National Register* reports that "the Cherokee deputation, composed of Field, Bushy head, Conrad, Woodward, and Pole Cat, are also on the *Santee* on their return to Washington." Apparently the Seminoles transferred from the *Camden* to the *Santee* at some point en route.[13]

Pickell relates one other relevant episode (November 30 and December 1); he does not name the vessel, but it could have been the *Santee*. Osceola, then a captive at St. Augustine, had asked to see his family. Pickell describes the family's arrival at Fort Mellon:

> They came with a white flag, hoisted upon a staff or pole 8 feet high and presented altogether a pitiable sight. The bearer of the flag was a fine looking young warrior and the head of the train, which was composed of about 50 souls including the two wives of Oseola and his two children & sister 3 warriors and the remainder negro men women & children. . . . they brought two miserable looking Indian ponies with them. From the voraciousness of their appetites when they were supplied with food, they seemed to have been nearly starved.

Lieutenant Pickell, as adjutant, was ordered to have twelve privates and two noncommissioned officers detailed to guard the retinue scheduled to leave for St. Augustine at reveille. The Seminoles seemed much surprised at the number of troops at Fort Mellon and were very reluctant to leave, as they did not relish the idea of going on board the "fire boat." Even Osceola's family manifested an indisposition to go to St. Augustine. Sprague records (May 25) that after Macomb's Indian agreement in May 1839 the general and his staff, on their way back to Washington, boarded Captain Brooks's steamboat for the 2½-day trip from Picolata to Wilmington (South Carolina). Brooks was described as a clever, gentlemanly man.

The last known adventure of the *Santee* occurred in 1840, when she figured in another rescue operation. Dr. Perrine, an early horticulturist who was residing with his family on Indian Key, was killed by the so-called Spanish Indians. Perrine's family was rescued and ended up with the Florida Squadron on the schooner *Flirt* under the command of Lieutenant McLaughlin of Camp Monroe battle fame. The *Flirt* headed into Cape Florida, where in a few days the Perrine family was picked up by the *Santee* and taken to St. Augustine. In 1850 the *Santee* was sold to an alien, having spent fifteen years in government charter and private service.[14] In retrospect it seems appropriate that the *Santee* — bearing the Indian tribal name first bequeathed to a community and river north of Charleston — should have a history so closely involved with the Seminoles and the Second Seminole War.

The fifteen-year lifespan of the *Santee* was longer than the six years averaged by contemporary Georgia steamboats, which were lightly constructed and subject to explosions, fire, and sinking. The *Cincinnati* was abandoned in 1848 (twelve years after construction), the *Forrester* after six years, and the *John Stoney* after ten years. On November 15, 1838, the *John McLean* was stranded and wrecked with no loss of life on the bar at New Smyrna; she was carrying Company H, Fourth Artillery, of Fort Mellon, which had just been relieved of its assignment to help build Fort Maitland. The *Charleston* apparently had the longest life: built in Charleston in 1837 it was not abandoned until 1876, after having been captured as a Confederate steamer and redocumented in 1863.[15]

Apart from the steamboat in Vinton's northwest view of Fort Mellon, the 1837 Greene & McGowran lithograph facing page 56 of John Lee Williams' *Territory of Florida* depicts a bow-end view of a steamboat at Volusia and thus gives some idea of the vessel's width. On the other hand, Vinton's drawing (showing the starboard side) gives an idea of the length. Both vessels show pairs of enclosed sidewheel paddles and adequate smokestacks.

Since the *Essayons* is included neither in the Senate audit of steamboats chartered nor in the list of early merchant steam vessels, it appears that she might have been a government boat. Noting that Motte referred to her as the *"U.S. Steamer Essayons"* and aware that *Essayons* is the motto of the army engineers, I contacted them. Their historical division was unaware of the *Essayons'* existence but did quickly uncover in the National Archives a pertinent letter dated July 13, 1839, from Lt. J. L. Hathaway, Charleston, to the War Department at Washington advising that the three boilers and a quantity of old iron mentioned in the sales of public property for the month of June 1839 were the old boilers and iron taken from the *"U.S. Steamer Essayons."* If the army did not refit the vessel with new boilers, her end must have come sometime in the first half of 1839. Perhaps General Scott would have felt a little less miserable if he had received a copy of Hathaway's letter. We know neither the date nor the place of her construction; since she experienced the same navigational problem the *Santee* at the Lake Monroe bar in 1936 with General Scott, and since lightly loaded she was able to assist the heavily loaded 169-ton *Camden*, she was probably comparable to the *Santee* in size and tonnage. Her only activity other than the incidents at Lake Monroe, Camp Monroe, and Lake George seems to have been some service on Black Creek in July 1836 (reported by Lieutenant Pickell and John Lee Williams) that involved ferrying troops and pursuing Indians.[16] Captain Peck of the *Essayons* may have been Fenn Peck, a Charleston and Savannah area mariner who between 1843 and 1846 commanded the *Gaston*, the *Cecile*, and the U.S. Army steamer *General Taylor* and who also became a noted Confederate blockade runner.[17]

The nine steamboats active at Fort Mellon thus were prominent among the vessels that made "the St. Johns alive with various crafts transporting supplies from its mouth to the everglades," as reported by a news correspondent from Tallahassee in November of 1837. Not only did they prepare the Sanford area for the advent of commercial steamboating some thirty-five years later, but they actually made a significant contribution to the war effort.[18]

Beyond this, it is incumbent to say that there has not been proper recognition of the extensive logistical employment of steamboats in the Second Seminole War, a first in American warfare and, perhaps, in warfare anywhere. George E. Buker in his *Swamp Sailors* states that "The experience and training gained by the officers and men of the United States Navy in the use of steamers during the Second Seminole War is overlooked by many naval historians."[19] But it should be pointed out that while the usage of steamboats on the St. Johns to Fort Mellon was obviously river oriented, it was not the riverine warfare of which Buker speaks. The St. Johns activity was logistical, best described by Jesup's goal of making the river "an avenue for transportation of troops and supplies near two hundred miles."[20] This activity of the army-operated steamboats, so neatly documented by Lieutenant Pickell, as well as that of the thirty-nine steamboats reported in other sectors of the war, conclusively demonstrates the first extensive logistical use of steamboats in warfare.

Similar logistical support in the war of 1812, such as for Andrew Jackson at the battle of New Orleans (the first steamboat having arrived at New Orleans in 1812), must have been minimal, because supplies were easily floated down the Mississippi on barges. On the other hand, the upstream course of the St. Johns from its mouth to Fort Mellon was not navigable by sailing vessels, rendering steamboats a necessity in 1837. John K. Mahon, though conceding a very small presence of steamboats in the War of 1812, says that "the full impact of the steamboat on war lay in the future."[21] It is obvious that the significant beginning of the "future" was about twenty-five years later, in the Second Seminole War in general and in particular at Fort Mellon.

Chapter 8
Fort Mellon Logistically —
The Satellite Forts —
The Post Returns

I have ... ordered General Eustis today to send five companies forward to reoccupy Fort Mellon, and prepare storehouses for the supplies for the campaign.

Gen. Thomas S. Jesup, November 4, 1837

It is reasonable to conjecture that if General Scott rather than General Jesup had been commanding in 1837, Fort Mellon might not have been the storehouse and supply center for the campaign. General Scott, before being recalled as commander of the Army of the South, had reconnoitered the St. Johns on the *Essayons* (April 24-29, 1836) closer to the Seminole strongholds. On a map entitled "A Map of the Seat of War in Florida 1836" found in the *American State Papers* (reproduced facing page 315 in Grant Foreman's *Indian Removal)* two designations appear: "Gen. Scott in SB Essayons" and "New Depot of Gen. Scott." The latter point Scott described as about eight miles below the southern end of Lake Monroe, which location became known as Fort Florida at Fort Florida Point on the St. Johns.[1] It lies near what John Bartram in 1766 named Bartram's Bluff; Bartram wrote of the "fine low dry bluff 4 foot above water" as being the "finest piece of rich dry ground I observed since we left the head of the river."[2] In the 1870-1930 era this site became a steamboat dock known as Fort Florida Landing. Mr. William Vincent, Sr., of Sanford has a log book of the *Osceola* (February 1, 1920-December 31, 1923) that registers stops at this landing; he also has a photograph of the landing taken about 1910. Cabell and Hanna mention Fort Florida in their book on the St. Johns River.[3] The location is now the property of Mr. A. D. McMillon. Access is by Fort Florida Road off Highway 17-92, about 1½ miles south of DeBary. It is noteworthy that of all the Fort Mellon satellite forts, this one, the least known then, is remembered today by way of Fort Florida Road. In any event, General Jesup had no love for General Scott, and given the more commodious dimensions of the Lake Monroe location it is not difficult to understand why Jesup preferred Camp Monroe (Fort Mellon).

Steamboat exploration was not

an end unto itself — as Pickell points out in his last entry (December 16, 1837), "we are now on the eve of another campaign." Jesup's campaign for 1837-38 hinged on the logistics of collecting forces and supplies at Fort Mellon, so that he would be able to move into the heart of the Seminole country to the south. The plan, as Jesup stated it on June 15, 1837, was that the army should operate in four columns, each being self-sufficient. The principal column would ascend the St. Johns, equipped with supplies, with steamboats and barges of light draft, and with the necessary land transportation to enable it "to keep the field for ten or fifteen days together."[4]

After he had been removed from duty in Florida, Jesup described his operations in his report of July 6, 1838, addressed to Secretary of War Poinsett. The general saw the theater of war in 1837 as a vast area extending over more than five degrees of latitude from Charlotte Harbor (Punta Gorda) up the Gulf coast to Cedar Keys and partly by way of the Suwanee to St. Augustine. To cover this three-hundred-mile area he reported that forty posts should be occupied during the campaign and that six separate army corps should cover an extent of at least one-hundred-fifty square miles. He considered the principal Indian force to be concentrated on the upper St. Johns, with several smaller bands roving north of Fort Mellon and Tampa Bay, and other bands spread over the country south to Florida Point (Cape Sable). It is evident from this report that in late 1837 Fort Mellon and the nearby satellite forts would have been among the forty posts involved — in fact, Jesup at this time specifically designated Fort Mellon as "the principal depot for the Army in the field."[5]

Surgeon Motte, a keen observer, noted that Jesup's plan was to divide the main wing of the army in Florida into four detachments, each strong enough to encounter the united force of the enemy. With a sufficient garrison left at each base for its defense, the detachments were to sweep down the peninsula by four different routes, "driving it," as Motte put it in a sporting phrase.[6] These four detachments, or columns, were directed toward the headwaters of the St. Johns. In Motte's *Journey to Wilderness,* maps on pages 171 and 179 show the routes of the two generals that Pickell also mentioned — General Hernandez between Indian River and the St. Johns and General Eustis to the west of the St. Johns. In addition to these four columns, three more were on the Florida west coast, making a total of seven, according to Mahon. The most important of the western forces was the one that started from Tampa Bay under Col. Zachary Taylor. In analyzing Jesup's campaign, Dr. Mahon, whose forte is military history, observes that the year before (1836) General Scott's campaign had its three wings of the center, left, and right, as Scott, thoroughly steeped in classic European methods of warfare, expressed it. Jesup's plan, entertaining seven columns, also proposed to trap the enemy between converging forces; Jesup did not, however, copy Scott in having each wing fire cannons at 11:00 A.M. each day to alert the others as to its location.[7]

Regardless of the number of wings, Fort Mellon in the fall of 1837 was the staging and funneling area for the St. Johns wing. Specifically, on November 4, 1837, Jesup authorized twenty thousand rations of subsistence and forage to be deposited there as soon as storehouses were ready. In his report to Poinsett, Jesup stated that he had desired to start operations on the first of October, because then more of the St. Johns would be navigable than at a later period, and he could avail himself of more than two months of service of the Florida troops, whose term of service expired in December. He also reported that the regular troops did not begin to arrive until the last of October and continued to come until December, with the principal volunteer force arriving about the first of December.[8]

On November 17 Eustis accordingly proceeded from Garey's Ferry to Fort Mellon, which Jesup had ordered him to reopen after the June 18 shutdown. Jesup accompanied General Eustis' command to Volusia and from there, joining the mounted dragoons under Colonel Twiggs, proceeded by land to Fort Mellon, where he arrived on November 26. Here Maj. William Lauderdale with five-hundred Tennessee volunteers was joined by General Hernandez, and the combined forces left for the head of the St. Johns upon the arrival of General Eustis at Fort Mellon.[9]

Pickell had only briefly alluded to these preparations when he wrote December 6 that General Jesup and his staff had left for Black Creek to organize the volunteer troops from Georgia, Alabama, and Tennessee. Actually, there was no lack of troops for Jesup, and they did require considerable organizing—this is borne out by his ambitious seven-pronged maneuvers. In Sprague's tabulations military forces in Florida for 1837 totaled eighty-four hundred, more by far than in any other year of the war. Mahon claims that the total was nearer nine thousand men.[10]

While the St. Johns wing made preparations, Zachary Taylor, having moved east from Tampa, was fighting the battle of Okeechobee on December 25, 1837. Mahon points out that at this time, "southward the four columns of the main wing of Jesup's army had drawn together under General Eustis. Numbering close to two thousand men, Eustis' command was directed from Fort Mellon on Lake Monroe. About ten miles south of it was Fort Lane, the center from which was directed the column of Florida militiamen."[11]

We have noted the efforts of

Lieutenant Pickell (under Colonel Bankhead) and Lieutenant Davidson (under Colonel Harney) to find a suitable post on Lake Harney; both Pickell (December 16) and Jesup report the movement of Major Dearborn from Fort Mellon to the same lake, Jesup in his official report:

> Major Dearborn was sent forward, with a detachment and supplies, in barges, to establish a depot at the head of Lake Harney [Fort Lane]; and General Eustis moved, with the principal force, by land. The country was so difficult that his march was necessarily slow. He erected Fort Christmas...on the 25th of December, and arrived on the 16th of January at Fort Taylor, a post about a hundred miles south of Fort Mellon, established by Colonel Twiggs, who had been sent in advance.
> Lieutenant Searle had been sent up the St. Johns to explore it; and Colonel Harney had followed with several barges loaded with forage. They ascertained the practicability of navigating the river to Fort Taylor.[12]

The above is graphically documented by an interesting sequence of Jesup's dispatches (December 18, 1837, to January 5, 1838) with the dateline "Headquarters Army of the South" changing as the general edged southward from "Fort Mellon" to "Fort Lane" to "Fort Christmas" to "Fort McNeil."[13]

South of Fort Mellon troops moved on foot, although some supplies, mostly fodder, were poled up the St. Johns on barges and flatboats. To move overland through the difficult terrain Jesup planned to have military posts about thirty miles apart. Fort Lane, the name of the post finally selected on Lake Harney (after Capt. John F. Lane, a West Pointer who had served with the Second Dragoons), is first mentioned in Jesup's dispatch datelined "Headquarters, Fort Lane, Head of Lake Harney, December 20, 1837." He and the dragoons had passed General Eustis, who was slogging along at the rate of about ten miles per day, having left Fort Mellon on the seventeenth. Jesup was concerned about the bar at the entrance to Lake Monroe and the necessity for a bridge to be built over the Econlockhatchee in connection with the move south from Fort Mellon. On December 22 Jesup issued one more dispatch from "Headquarters, Army of the South, Fort Lane, Head of Lake Harney" in which he said: "The dragoons are employed to day in packing forage forward. The Tennesseeans, and the few Floridians still in service, are opening a road from this post to General Eustis's camp, south; and the artillery, under the immediate command of the general, are erecting a bridge over Ecowlaik Hatchee [Econlockhatchee]. Lieutenant Searle went forward this morning, with a Mackinac boat loaded with forage, to ascertain whether the navigation be practicable above."[14]

The stepping stones next after Fort Lane were Fort Christmas (December 30; January 2) and Fort McNeil (January 5). Jesup's dispatches are interesting in that they illustrate how army headquarters moved with the commanding general during the Second Seminole War. At the time of the December 30 dispatch Fort Christmas was only five days old; it had been built eighty feet square of pine pickets with two substantial blockhouses twenty feet square. The dispatches also testify to the slow progress of the army, which had to make its own roads and bridges as it moved — as Dr. Mahon points out, "the supply line stretched out precariously as the army moved southward. Volusia lost its importance as a supply point, then Fort Mellon, then even Fort Lane."[15] Fort Lane's tenure as "Headquarters Army of the South" was indeed brief, as Samuel Forry, an army surgeon, reported on March 4, 1838: "By yesterdays express we also learned that this post [Fort Taylor] and Fort Lane are to be abandoned in several weeks." On his visit to Fort Mellon and Fort Kingsbury in 1839, Sprague wrote: "Fort Lane is on Lake Harney, 30 miles above Ft. Mellon, but at present unoccupied."[16] The fort had already served its purpose as a stepping stone to the south.

The official records of Fort Lane, the so-called "post returns," are essentially attendance reports for the months of December (1837), January, and February (1838); during these three months the total averaged almost 125 men, including a fifer and a drummer. The detachment of Second Infantry was under the command of Bvt. Maj. Greenleaf Dearborn, and the adjutant and commissary officer in charge of subsistence was 1st Lt. Silas Casey, according to the entries made by the latter. Casey was later a captain in Colonel Lane's Creek regiment. Other officers present were second lieutenants J. R. D. Bennett and William Alburtis. Lieutenant Hannibal Day was listed as absent because of being on recruiting service; Bvt. Maj. Thomas Staniford was also reported as absent — he was commanding a battalion of recruits at Fort Mellon by order (December 14) of Lieutenant Colonel Bankhead. According to Motte, when the troops under Eustis left Fort Mellon, Staniford remained with a garrison of 140 men. Motte was also personally acquainted with Major Dearborn, whom he described as of large stature and from Maine; he likened the major's appetite to that of Don Quixote's squire, Sancho Panza, and reported his speed in swallowing as greater than a steamboat going downstream.[17]

Fort Lane appears on the Mackay and Blake map of 1840, a copy of which is the frontispiece to the January 1927 issue of the *Florida Historical Quarterly* and appears on an 1846 map of Orange County. Charles Coe, in an appendix to his *Red Patriots*, locates Fort Lane on the western shore of Lake Harney and classifies it as "temporary"; Heitman lists it as on the "St..Johns River, near Lake Harney."[18] Today the location of Fort Lane is marked by the Geneva Historical and Genealogical Society's Fort Lane Park, a beautiful and well-kept facility that may be reached by taking Lake Harney Road about two miles east of Geneva off State Highway 46. Neither Fort Mellon nor any of the other satellite forts is maintained and preserved as a historical location. (There is now recently completed a replica of Fort Christmas, but for security and maintenance reasons it is located in a county park about two miles from the actual site of the fort.)

Lieutenant Davidson recounts that on January 3, 1838, General Jesup himself led a column of seventy wagons and one thousand horses (the St. Johns wing) southward from Fort Christmas (on present Route 50, south of Sanford), which was garrisoned by nine companies of the Third Artillery under Major Lomax. General Jesup, who had been with the column since it left Fort Mellon, directed its movements until it reached Fort Taylor on the sixth of January, when having received intelligence the day before the battle of Okeechobee, he started with eight companies of dragoons to join Zachary Taylor. On January 18 the St. Johns wing along with General Eustis made contact with Colonel Taylor; six days later Jesup was able to reap some glory for his converging column strategy in the battle of the Loxahatchee.[19] By his own request Jesup was finally able to terminate his command after eighteen months and was succeeded by Taylor on May 18, 1838.

Despite the lake in the immediate Sanford vicinity named after him, Jesup is not very well remembered in America or in Florida. Of the seven top generals in the musical chairs game played by the War Department in the Second Seminole War, most Americans today remember only two—Taylor for the battle of Okeechobee (and for being president) and Scott for what he did long after he had left Florida.[20]

Of the march under General Eustis that left Fort Mellon on December 18 and arrived twenty days later at Jupiter Inlet, an anonymous officer of the expedition asserted that it was

one of the most extraordinary marches ever made in this or any other country, considering the obstacles to be overcome. For nearly two hundred miles we passed through an unknown region, cutting roads through dense hummocks, passing innumerable cypress-swamps and pine-barrens, interspersed with a nearly impassable growth of saw palmetto, and, for the last three days, wading nearly up to our waists in water. Our privations have not been less than our fatigue, the men being almost naked, and one third of them destitute of shoes.

64

Another officer of the Second Dragoons said:

> Our march from Fort Mel-
> lon to the southern portion of Florida was marked by ... a great
> destruction of the finest horses that I have ever seen. Our regiment
> suffered a great loss — one that I fear will not be made up in some
> time; nearly the whole is now mounted, but on indifferent hor-
> ses.[21]

These were the same dragoons who had arrived at Jacksonville on
October 31 in prime condition after fifty-five days traveling twelve
hundred miles overland from St. Louis.[22] Clearly the Florida frontier in
1837-38 had a setting all its own.

From the description of these
exhausting marches it can be seen that "the logistical failure was a failure
in transportation, not in supply; the depots had been adequately stocked
by the Commissary General of Subsistence, but wagons, roads, and
Army maps were lacking."[23] This conclusion pertained to General
Scott's 1836 campaign; yet the same essentially held true the following
year. Actually, the existence of Fort Mellon in 1837, by its closer proxim-
ity to the retreating Seminoles, expedited transportation as far as Lake
Monroe; beyond that point, however, it was again the old "immense
baggage train" pushing through impenetrable terrain. Fort Mellon as a
depot also adequately played its role as a supply station. Logistically,
then, Fort Mellon functioned as the staging area for the St. Johns wing of
the 1837-38 campaign and contributed to the battles of Okeechobee and
the Loxahatchee.

The war in 1838 south of Fort
Mellon can be followed in Motte's *Journey*. Although Jesup did not end
the war, it was under his command that the majority of the Seminole
chiefs along with their people and slaves were killed, kidnapped, or
persuaded to go to their new reservations.[24] Hostilities did continue after
Jesup left but on a much reduced scale.

Further information about Fort
Mellon is provided by the post returns. Army regulations required the
commanding officer of every post, as well as commanders of such lesser
groups as brigades, regiments, and detachments, to submit a return or
personnel report at specified intervals to the adjutant general. Basically,
this return listed the units that were stationed at a particular post and
their strength, the names and duties of the officers, and the number of
officers present and absent and recorded official communications and
events. In general, the returns for a specific post cover the period of
official existence. The Fort Mellon post returns run from March 1837 to

April 1842, although as with many other posts there are gaps in dates. For Fort Mellon there are no returns for the periods June-October 1837; April-September 1838; March and August-December 1839; all of 1840; and August-October 1841. Usually officers are listed in descending order of rank.[25]

The following tabulation of the Fort Mellon post returns shows what troops were present, gives the aggregate force, and identifies the commanding officer and the other commissioned officers.

March 1837. Second Dragoons; Second and Third Artillery. 364.
Lt. Col. W. S. Harney, Second Dragoons. J. R. Vinton, J. L. Bean, S. H. Anderson, W. B. Davidson, John Graham, Townshend Dade, M. S. Howe, G. A. H. Blake, R. H. Peyton, J. W. S. McNeil, C. E. Kingsbury, C. A. May (nine officers absent).

April 1837. Second Dragoons; Second and Third Artillery. 304.
Lt. Col. W. S. Harney, Second Dragoons. C. H. Laub (assistant surgeon), J. R. Vinton, S. H. Anderson, W. B. Davidson, John Graham, M. S. Howe, G. A. H. Blake, R. H. Peyton, Samuel Bransford, J. W. S. McNeil, C. E. Kingsbury, C. A. May (nine officers absent).

May 1837. Second Dragoons; Second and Third Artillery. 299.
Lt. Col. W. S. Harney, Second Dragoons. C. H. Laub (assistant surgeon), S. H. Anderson, W. B. Davidson, John Graham, M. S. Howe, G. A. H. Blake, R. H. Peyton, J. W. S. McNeil, C. E. Kingsbury, Samuel Bransford (eleven officers absent).

(Summer slowdown: June through October)

November 1837. Detachment of Second Infantry, 127.
Bvt. Maj. Greenleaf Dearborn. Thomas Staniford, Silas Casey, I. R. D. Burnett, William Alburtis (one officer absent).

———— Second Dragoons (field return). 384.
Col. David Twiggs. W. S. Harney, Thomas Fauntleroy, Samuel De-Camp (assistant surgeon), William Tompkins, Edward Winder, William Fulton, Lloyd Beall, John Graham, Townshend Dade, E. D. Bullock, George Forsyth, N. W. Hunter, Robert Lawton, Nathan Darling, Louis Craig, John Parker.

———— Battalion of Fourth Artillery (encamped near Fort Mellon). 189.
Bvt. Maj. J. L. Gardner, companies A, D, and H. E. C. Ross, S. B. Dusenberry, T. L. Brent, Edmund Bradford, Thomas Williams, J. C. Pemberton, W. T. Martin (eight officers absent).

———— Company B of Fourth Artillery. 65.
Capt. J. M. Washington. J. P. J. O'Brien, George Thomas (three officers absent).

December 1837. Battalion of recruits (encamped near Fort Mellon). 184.
Two companies of recruits. 115.
Bvt. Maj. Thomas Staniford, Third Infantry. Charles Collins, George Watson, C. H. Laub (assistant surgeon), Robert Allen, F. O. Wyse.

January 1838. Two companies of recruits. 115.
Bvt. Maj. Thomas Staniford, Second Infantry. Charles Collins, George Watson, C. H. Laub (assistant surgeon), Robert Allen, George Taylor, E. J. Steptoe, F. O. Wyse.

February 1838. Two companies of recruits. 114.
Bvt. Maj. Thomas Staniford, Second Infantry. Charles Collins, George Watson, C. H. Laub (assistant surgeon), Robert Allen, George Taylor, F. O. Wyse.

March 1838. Detachment of Second Regiment of Second Infantry. 301.
Bvt. Maj. Greenleaf Dearborn. E. D. Bullock, Silas Casey, M. S. Howe, Charles Collins, George Watson, William Gilpin, J. R. D. Bennett, William Alburtis, C. H. Laub (assistant surgeon).

(Summer slowdown: April through September)

October 1838. Troops. 373.
Lt. Col. A. C. W. Fanning, Fourth Artillery. J. H. Miller, D. H. Tufts, G. F. Turner (assistant surgeon), Charles Noyes (assistant surgeon), Harvey Brown, E. C. Ross, F. E. Hunt, A. E. Shiras, W. G. Freeman, J. P. J. O'Brien, J. W. Phelps, T. L. Brent, Thomas Williams, J. R. Soley, T. L. Ringgold, J. W. Gunnison (twelve officers absent).

*November 1838. Companies D and I of Fourth Artillery; Company C of Second Dragoons. 204.
Lt. A. E. Shiras, Fourth Artillery. T. L. Ringgold, F. E. Hunt, T. L. Brent, Lloyd Beall, Owen Ransom, G. F. Turner (assistant surgeon), Charles Noyes (assistant surgeon) (five officers absent).

†December 1838. Troops. 128.
Bvt. Maj. J. L. Gardner, Fourth Artillery. E. C. Ross, A. E. Shiras, T. L. Ringgold, G. F. Turner (assistant surgeon), F. E. Hunt, T. L. Brent, Charles Noyes (assistant surgeon) (three officers absent).

COMMISSIONED OFFICERS of the Post, present and absent, accounted for.

Commissioned Officers are required to be accounted for, *by name;* and will be classed and arranged according to the following order : 1st. "**Present at the Post** ;" 2d. "**Absent** ;" as those who may be on "*Staff duty* ;" "*Recruiting Service* ;" "*Ordnance duty* ;" "*Topographical duty* ;" "*Other special duty* ;" "*On furlough* ;" "*Without leave* ;" &c.

No.	NAMES.	RANK.	REGIMENT.	Letters of Companies.	REMARKS. "The reasons for, and the time," (date of the order,) which any Officer attached to the Garrison, may be absent from his Post, will be specified.
	PRESENT AT THE POST				
1	A. E. Shiras	1st Lt.	4 Art.	D	Com'd Comp. & Comm. & Act'g Q.M. at Fort Mellon
2	T. L. Ringgold	2d Lt.	"	"	Com'd Detach'd at Fort Maitland 14 miles from Ft. Mellon
3	F. E. Hunt	1st Lt.	"	I	Com'd the Comp. and Ord'd to Fort Gatlin
4	T. L. Brent	2d Lt.	"	"	Ass't Comm. & Act'g Ass't Q.M. at Fort Gatlin
5	Lloyd S. Beall	Capt.	2d Drag	C	Com'd his Comp. at Fort Mellon
6	Owen Ransom	2d Lt.	"	"	Joined fr. Charleston Station 17 Nov. 1838
7	G. F. Turner	Ass't Surg.	—	.	Fort Mellon
8	C. Noyes	—	—		Fort Gatlin
	Absent				
1	Samuel Cooper	Capt.	4 Art.	D	Ass't Adj. General
2	E. C. Ross	1st Lt.	"	"	" On leave at Geary's Ferry for 7 days by order of Maj. Gardner
3	John Erving	Capt.	"	I	Leave of absence—sick—Sept. 1 ord. Oct. 21. 1838
4	F. Searle	1st Lt.	"	"	Ass't Q.M. at Fort Butler
5	N. Darling	1st Lt.	2 Drag	C	A. C. S. Comm. at Fort Butler &c.

November 1838.

The Fort Mellon Post Return for November 1838. (National Archives)

†January 1839. Troops. 126.
   Bvt. Maj. J. L. Gardner, Fourth Artillery. E. C. Ross, A. E. Shiras, T. L. Ringgold, G. F. Turner (assistant surgeon), F. E. Hunt, T. L. Brent, Charles Noyes (assistant surgeon) (three officers absent).

†February 1839. Troops. 125.
   Bvt. Maj. J. L. Gardner, Fourth Artillery. E. C. Ross, A. E. Shiras, F. E. Hunt, T. L. Brent, G. F. Turner (assistant surgeon), Charles Noyes (assistant surgeon) (four officers absent).

(March 1839: no report. According to Sprague, Gardner, Turner, and Shiras were still at Fort Mellon as of April 9.)

April 1839. Troops. 52.
   1st Lt. W. K. Hanson, Seventh Infantry. R. F. Baker (two officers absent).

May 1839. Troops. 51.
   1st Lt. W. K. Hanson, Seventh Infantry. R. F. Baker (two officers absent).

June 1839. Troops. 48.
   1st Lt. W. K. Hanson, Seventh Infantry. R. F. Baker (two officers absent).

July 1839. Troops. 49.
1st Lt. W. K. Hanson, Seventh Infantry. Charles Noyes (assistant surgeon), R. F. Baker (two officers absent).

(August 1839 to December 1840: no report)

January 1841. Company B of Second Dragoons. 66.
Capt. William Fulton. Ephraim Thayer (one officer absent).

February 1841. Company B of Second Dragoons. 64.
Capt. William Fulton. William McKissack, Ephraim Thayer (one officer absent).

March 1841. Company B of Second Dragoons. 63.
Capt. William Fulton. William McKissack, Ephraim Thayer (one officer absent).

April 1841. Company B of Second Dragoons. 63.
Lt. Ephraim Thayer. William McKissack, William Hoxton (assistant surgeon) (two officers absent).

May 1841. Company B of Second Dragoons. 62.
Capt. William Fulton. William Hoxton (assistant surgeon), Ephraim Thayer (one officer absent).

June 1841. Company H of Second Dragoons. 58.
Capt. N. W. Hunter. W. H. Hammond (assistant surgeon), O. F. Winship (two officers absent).

July 1841. Company C of Second Dragoons. 68.
Lt. L. P. Graham. O. F. Winship, Samuel Moore (assistant surgeon) (one officer absent).

(Summer slowdown: August through October)

November 1841. Company G of Second Infantry. 77.
Capt. E. K. Barnum. S. P. Moore (assistant surgeon), Julius Hayden (one officer absent).

December 1841. Company G of Second Infantry. 74.
Capt. E. K. Barnum. S. P. Moore (assistant surgeon), G. W. Patten, Julius Hayden.

January 1842. Company G of Second Infantry. 74.
Capt. E. K. Barnum. Lyman Foot (surgeon), G. W. Patten, Julius Hayden.

69

February 1842. Company G of Second Infantry. 73.
Capt. E. K. Barnum. Joseph Walker (assistant surgeon), G. W. Patten (one officer absent).

March 1842. Company G of Second Infantry. 73.
Capt. E. K. Barnum. Joseph Walker (assistant surgeon), G. W. . Patten (one officer absent).

April 1842. Company G of Second Infantry. 76.
Capt. E. K. Barnum. Joseph Walker (assistant surgeon), G. W. Patten (one officer absent).

*Includes personnel for Fort Gatlin
†Includes personnel for Fort Gatlin and Fort Maitland

Observation of the personnel for March, April, and May of 1837 reveals that essentially the old February battle group of dragoons was back under Harney. Fanning's "retrograde" movement down the river to Volusia (Astor) after the battle was only temporary. The new officers not present at the battle were Anderson, Bransford, Dade, and Peyton. Kingsbury and McNeil, on the other hand, are absent. The former died of fever in June, as Motte noted on his visit; his name was given to the temporary fort across the lake from Fort Mellon. McNeil, at nineteen, was the youngest officer to be lost when he was a casualty in October near Fort Peyton.

In the March return Harney noted that he had left Fort Call (Astor) to reoccupy Fort Mellon on March 8, 1837, with four companies of dragoons, six companies of the Second and Third Artillery, three companies of South Carolina militia and 128 Creek volunteers, as ordered by General Jesup. In April the South Carolina volunteers and Company C of the Second Dragoons reported two deaths by cholera, one by dysentery, and one by accidental discharge of a firearm. Second Lieutenant May (no doubt due to his bottom rank) was absent in the month of May on detail service driving cattle to St. Augustine.

The ambitious plans evidenced by the large aggregate forces in the spring of 1837 were thwarted by the summer slowdown — not until November and December did the forces reach previous levels. In November each body of troops, it will be noted, was making separate returns. The detachment of Second Infantry under Dearborn was the same group that was sent to occupy Fort Lane from December 1837 through February 1838 and that returned to Fort Mellon in March of 1838. George C. Thomas, who fired the cannon on the *Santee*, appears in the November report of the Fourth Artillery. His company B had left Picolata on November 17 and had arrived at Fort Mellon on the eighteenth, a trip that Pickell anticipated in his journal entry of November 16, 1837. Then and three days later Pickell mentioned lieutenants Allen, Ross, Martin, and Tompkins as well as Major Gardner, all names that appear in the returns. Of the two companies of recruits reporting in December, Staniford listed twelve confined to the hospital. Staniford also noted that the recruits had been accompanied from Black Creek by lieutenants Allen and Lincoln, a point confirmed by Pickell (November 30). It is odd that Pickell and his commanding officer, Lieutenant Colonel Bankhead, are not included in the Fort Mellon post returns. Of course, they were on an exploration detail; however, Bankhead was cited in the January 1838 post return of Fort Lane as having issued an order in December at Fort Mellon.

Although the post returns list routine military matters, there is never a mention of Cherokees or Seminoles, nor exploration, nor steamboats. Were it not for Pickell and Motte, our picture of Fort Mellon would be quite drab. The post returns do not even mention the massive December 1837 evacuation of troops under generals Eustis, Hernandez, and Jesup, though this is evident from the drop in aggregate forces for January, February, and March of 1838. The March return notes Dearborn's return to Fort Mellon by stating that the detachment "embarked at Fort Lane, Fla. 16th March 1838 and arrived at Fort Mellon the same day." Apparently its chief assignment was one of livery duty: Jesup's only command to the fort at this time seems to have been order 69 (March 10, 1838) instructing that the dragoon horses sent to Fort Mellon be retained there and be attended to with utmost care.

A summer shutdown again occurred in 1838, there being no returns for April through September. Jesup's order 116 (May 13, 1838) had authorized the withdrawal of troops and stores from Fort Mellon to Black Creek.[26] By October, however, the garrison was back to strength under the Camp Monroe battle commander, Fanning, who was to be occupied with these items he listed under "Remarks": "Col. Fanning to reestablish Fort Mellon; Fort Gatlin to be established." In general order 98 (November 18, 1838), Brevet Major Gardner was placed in command of forts Mellon and Gatlin, with his headquarters at Fort Mellon. Another letter order (November 29, 1838) "directs the new Out Post 14 miles from Ft. Mellon to be called *Fort Maitland* and requires a Sergeant General there from troops at Ft. Mellon."

The listing of commissioned officers for November 1838 shows how the duties at Fort Mellon were assigned. Lieutenant Shiras was posted to Fort Mellon; Ringgold was detailed at Fort Maitland "14 miles from Ft. Mellon"; Hunt was in charge of the "Out Post 'Fort Gatlin'"; Brent was the quartermaster at Fort Gatlin; and Turner and Noyes were assistant surgeons at Fort Mellon and Fort Gatlin respectively. In December and January the first five names on the staff are bracketed for Fort Mellon and the last three — Hunt, Brent, and Noyes — for Fort Gatlin. As to the Fourth Artillery, Company D was at forts Mellon and Maitland and Company I at Fort Gatlin. In February 1839 Gardner, Ross, Shiras, and Turner are indicated for Fort Mellon and Hunt, Brent, and Noyes for Fort Gatlin. In December, January, and February the post returns for Fort Mellon are captioned as including forts Gatlin and Maitland.

After February the post was lightly garrisoned by the Seventh Infantry and had little to report apart from occasional references to the two satellite forts. In April the privates of D Company were detailed to occupy Fort Maitland, and in July Assistant Surgeon Noyes "joined from post at Fort Gatlin," which post it was announced was to be evacuated. An unrelated order prohibited the practice of cutting live oak. July ends the post returns for 1839 and the reports of forts Gatlin and Maitland.

The official Fort Gatlin post returns (November 1838-June 1839) reflect the information contained in the Fort Mellon post returns of October 1838 to July 1839 regarding Fort Gatlin. For the five months from November 1838 through March 1839 the Fort Gatlin post returns show Hunt as commander, Noyes as assistant surgeon, and Brent as assistant commissary of subsistence and assistant quartermaster. The November returns state that Colonel Fanning with companies A, B, H, and I of the Fourth Artillery arrived (from Fort Mellon) and commenced building Fort Gatlin, E.F., on the ninth and that Fanning left Fort Gatlin with Companies A, B, and H on the fifteenth while Company I under the command of Lt. F. E. Hunt remained to garrison the post. In March Brent was reported absent for five days on scouting duty at Lake Apopka, and in April the fort received a district order regarding the transporting of rations to the Indians.

For the balance of Fort Gatlin's existence — April, May, and June 1839 — Noyes continued as assistant surgeon, but the Second Dragoon officers were represented by Capt. William M. Fulton, commander, and Lt. William Joseph Hardee, an 1838 graduate of West Point, who served as assistant commissary of subsistence and assistant quartermaster. (The Fort Mellon returns show that Fulton later commanded Fort Mellon for four months in 1841.) In the Fort Gatlin Post Return for June is found general order 28 (June 22, 1839) relating to the abandoning of the fort. The average aggregate force for the eight months had been sixty-four. After a lapse of ten years, there appears one last Fort Gatlin Post Return, for October 1849. Captain Israel Vogdes of the First Artillery occupied and assumed command of the post on October 26; he was assisted by eight other officers, of whom six (as well as himself) were graduates of the U.S. Military Academy. The aggregate force was 113. Apparently this activity was the beginning of what dragged on into the 1850s as the Third Seminole War.[27]

        There are no separate post returns for Fort Maitland. The last report concerning this fort appears in the April 1839 Fort Mellon Post Return, which suggests that Fort Maitland was occupied only from October 1838 to April 1839. As is generally known, Fort Maitland became the city of Maitland (as Fort Christmas became Christmas); Fort Gatlin, however, did not end up as Gatlin (nor even as Jernigan, later applied to the area) but as the city of Orlando. The city does have a Lake Gatlin and a Gatlin Avenue.

        Returning to Fort Mellon, we find an episode not reported in the returns: Sprague relates that in July 1839 General Macomb and the Seminoles had agreed upon a trading post to be established near the mouth of the Caloosahatchee River on the west coast. A small force under Colonel Harney was sent to give protection while the post was being built; when Indians made a surprise attack, about half of this force was killed, but Harney escaped. As a result Lieutenant Hanson was directed by General Taylor to ready the defenses of Fort Mellon against a possible attack; rather oddly, he also was ordered to withdraw his detachment of forty-nine. Before leaving Fort Mellon, Hanson did seize forty-six Seminoles then visiting his post to obtain provisions, though in fact the Indians on the southwest coast had not been a party to the trading post agreement. Sprague observed that Hanson's command, though small, effected this action in a most skillful manner and shipped the Seminoles immediately to Charleston, whence they were sent to Arkansas.[28]

        For the first half of 1841 the Dragoons were back in charge with a small force — the January post return states that "Captain Fulton occupied Fort Mellon E.F. January 1, 1841 pursuant to District Order No. 48 dated Headquarters St. Johns District, Fort Reid E.F. December 31, 1840." (This entry is further discussed in chapter 9.) In June Capt. Nathaniel Wyche Hunter was in command with fifty-eight men; though a West Point graduate, Hunter was critical of the military in general, as revealed in his diaries, and of Fort Mellon in particular — he said that those responsible for the fort's flimsy defenses should be ashamed to call it a military post. Construction, no doubt, would have followed General Jesup's order 73 (March 15, 1838) wherein he advised that the barracks at Tampa Bay should be built of logs covered with shingles or clapboards, whichever was more convenient or economical. The August 1841 post return does not reveal the official army policy of retrenchment and rigid economy; at Fort Mellon, however, one civilian cartman was discharged, and though citizen clerks were employed elsewhere at $75 per month, at Fort Mellon the assistant commissary of subsistence was also acting as assistant quartermaster, for which extra services it was necessary to pay only $20 per month additional.[29]

From November 1841 to April 1842 (the last post return for Fort Mellon) Capt. E. K. Barnum of the Second Infantry commanded. He and Fort Mellon were prominent in one of the many actions initiated by Col. W. J. Worth, who took over the Florida command from Armistead in May 1841; Worth (Sprague's father-in-law) was attempting to clean up the few remaining small bands of roving Indians, one of them the remnant group of Halleck Tustenugee believed to be in the neighborhood of New Smyrna in November 1841. To scout them out, a force from Fort King and Palatka was to proceed to Fort Mellon and take all but twenty of that garrison's seventy-seven men; from Fort Mellon it was to proceed to New Smyrna, relying mostly upon packing mules for conveying its twelve to fifteen days' provision. (Captain Barnum was to be the backup officer in the event that the designated commander for the scouting maneuver should be unable to report.) From Smyrna the force was to scout as far south as Fort Pierce, replenish provisions there, and then return to Fort Mellon.[30]

Halleck Tustenugee, however, was not found in New Smyrna, and it was not until April 1842 that other forces finally captured him — he reacted by saying, "I have been hunted like a wolf and now I am about to be sent away like a dog."[31] It is significant that this action, the last one of the war to be considered a battle, just about coincides with the end of Fort Mellon's official life. According to Hamersly's *Army Register,* the fort was officially abandoned May 27, 1842,[32] not quite 5½ years after the February 11, 1837, detachment order read by Fanning at the burial rites of Captain Mellon.

Chapter 9
Fort Reid and Mellonville

The post [Fort Reid] was named by Col. Harney after the present governor of Florida.

Bvt. Maj. J. A. Ashby, Fort Reid, November 1840

Fort Reid had been established on July 7, 1840. The November Fort Reid Post Return explains why there were no Fort Mellon post returns for 1840: "Fort Reid is about a mile and a half directly west of Fort Mellon; this latter post being only used as a landing place for the former; the post was named by Col. Harney after the present Governor of Florida." This statement by Major Ashby also enables us to determine the correct spelling of the fort's name. Robert Raymond Reid was from 1840 to 1841 the fourth governor of the unified territory of Florida. A South Carolinian born in 1789, he was educated and practiced law in Augusta, Georgia. As a talented public speaker he served Georgia in congress and as a judge of various courts. In 1832 Andrew Jackson appointed him United States judge of East Florida, in which capacity he remained until December 1839 when Van Buren appointed him governor of Florida. Reid also presided at the convention that drafted the Florida Constitution. He died of yellow fever in the summer of 1841 at the plantation of his son-in-law, Lt. John Graham.[1]

A statement by Governor Reid cited in John A. Sullivan's 1976 *Florida Historical Calendar* suggests that the army named Fort Reid after him in recognition of his vigorous advocacy of the war, for he claimed that "the situation in Florida is worse than it ever has been." Reid had written to the secretary of war recommending that the War Department send 3,000 military horsemen to defend against Seminole attacks in East Florida.[2] Another instance of the army's deference to Reid was the special order General Armistead issued on November 21, 1840, whereby Lt. R. A. Arnold (listed in the July, August, and October post returns of Fort Reid) was assigned to command the escort of Governor Reid from Garey's Ferry to Tallahassee.[3] Reid's name was further perpetuated in Florida history by his widow, who was active in hospital work in behalf of sick and wounded Florida men during the Civil War. In recognition of her efforts the first Florida unit of the United Daughters of the Confederacy was named the Mary Martha Reid Chapter.[4]

Sprague in his *Florida War* mentions twelve deaths at Fort Reid between September 8, 1840, and February 16, 1841. The same spelling was also used 100 years ago by Sidney Lanier in describing the settlements around Sanford.[5] The apparently preferred local spelling "Read" reflects the name of Col. Leigh Read, in whose honor there had been an abortive 1838 attempt to change the name of Mosquito County to Leigh Read County. Read was a controversial figure who attacked Gen. Winfield Scott verbally, killed a man in a duel, and was himself killed by an avenger.[6] "Reed," another local spelling, received official sanction when there subsequently was established near the fort a post office, the name of which was requested by petition to be "Fort Reed."[7]

Fort Reid's existence first was implied in General Armistead's order 23 (June 28, 1840), in which the regiments were instructed to take up positions in order to protect the settlements, with four companies of the Second Dragoons being assigned to the "post near Fort Mellon." In the same order Colonel Twiggs was designated as commanding the eastern district composed of the Second Dragoons, the Third Artillery, and the Second and Seventh regiments of infantry. He was also instructed to retain command of the troops east of the Suwanee and to place his "Head Quarters at some point admitting of a rapid and easy communication with the different stations." Lieutenant Colonel Harney was assigned "to the command of a sub-district comprising the country east of the St. Johns and south of and including New Smyrna."

Definite identification of Colonel Twiggs's headquarters is provided by Armistead's orders 57 and 58 of November 15, 1840, wherein Twiggs and two companies of Second

Dragoons were instructed to "repair to Fort Reid. . . to scour the country from Fort Reid to the Ocklawaha. . . to the annoyance and destruction of the enemy." The specific title of Colonel Twiggs's command is spelled out in Armistead's special order 84 of November 28, 1840: "During the continuance of active operations the Head Quarters of the St. Johns district will be established at Fort Reid."[8]

The following tabulation of the Fort Reid post returns shows how many companies of the Second Dragoons were present, gives the aggregate force, and identifies the commanding officer and the other commissioned officers.

July 1840. Four companies. 276.
    Capt. G. A. H. Blake. W. S. Harney, S. P. Moore (acting assistant surgeon), Croghan Ker, N. W. Hunter, R. A. Arnold, W. H. Saunders, Albert Lowry (seven officers absent).

August 1840. Four companies. 264.
    Captain G. A. H. Blake (sick). W. S. Harney, S. P. Moore (acting assistant surgeon), Joseph Walker (assistant surgeon), Croghan Ker, Robert Lawton, R. A. Arnold, W. H. Saunders (nine officers absent).

September 1840. Three companies. 192.
    Captain G. A. H. Blake. Croghan Ker, Joseph Walker (assistant surgeon) (ten officers absent).

October 1840. Four companies reported (six actually present). 416.
    Capt. Croghan Ker. W. S. Harney, Joseph Walker (acting assistant surgeon), G. A. H. Blake, William Fulton, H. H. Sibley, Z. M. P. Inge, R. A. Arnold, W. H. Saunders (eight officers absent).

November 1840. Six companies. 410.
    Bvt. Maj. J. A. Ashby. William McKissack, Joseph Walker (assistant surgeon), William Fulton, Croghan Ker, H. H. Sibley, N. W. Hunter, Nathan Darling, Z. M. P. Inge, Albert Lowry, Ephraim Thayer (eleven officers absent).

December 1840. Six companies. 417.
    Maj. Thomas Fauntleroy. William McKissack, R. S. Satterlee (surgeon), Joseph Walker (assistant surgeon), David Twiggs, R. C. Asheton, J. A. Ashby, William Fulton, Croghan Ker, N. W. Hunter, Owen Ransom, H. H. Sibley, Z. M. P. Inge, Albert Lowry, Ephraim Thayer, Fowler Hamilton, R. P. Campbell.

January 1841. Five companies. 344.

Bvt. Maj. J. A. Ashby. R. S. Satterlee (surgeon), Joseph Walker (assistant surgeon), William McKissack, David Twiggs, R. C. Asheton, Croghan Ker, Owen Ransom, H. H. Sibley, Z. M. P. Inge, Fowler Hamilton, R. P. Campbell (five officers absent).

Fort Reid was heavily garrisoned for the seven months of its official reporting tenure; the 1839, 1841, and 1842 returns of Fort Mellon, on the other hand, indicate much lighter forces there. The Second Dragoons was the only regiment present, but its top officers were well represented. In the returns from July through October Colonel Harney was not in command of the post but was listed as "Commanding the district south of New Smyrna." Colonel Twiggs, listed on the staff for December and January, was described as "Commanding the Regiment and St. Johns District Army of Florida"; and in numerous dispatches from Fort Reid, Colonel Twiggs indicated this post as "Head Quarters 2nd Dragoons."

During the period (April-May 1840) between the Florida War commands of Zachary Taylor and General Armistead, Colonel Twiggs, as senior officer, was installed as temporary commander in Florida. Armistead, after taking over, divided Florida into two command zones, placing Twiggs in command of the eastern section. This, no doubt, is why Fort Reid was so heavily garrisoned: it was the headquarters of the St. Johns District under Colonel Twiggs and the district south of New Smyrna under Harney; but why Fort Mellon could not have assumed the burden of this additional responsibility is not clear. Perhaps the commanders of the two districts wanted a unique command post to implement the new authority. Or perhaps the condition of the Fort Mellon buildings as reported by Captain Hunter precluded their use as a base for the new district commanders.

Thus Fauntleroy, Twiggs, and Harney, the top three officers of the Second Dragoons, were on the staff at Fort Reid, as were original dragoons Ashby and Ker, who commanded the post. We also see John Alexander Hamilton Blake, three times commander of Fort Reid, on his way to a long military career starting with his citation by Colonel Fanning at the battle of Camp Monroe.

In the January return Ashby noted that the "garrison was reduced on the 1st inst. by the withdrawal of B Co. Agg. 66 to Fort Mellon post by order of Colonel D. E. Twiggs." Correspondingly Company B, with aggregate force of 66, was entered in the January 1841 Fort Mellon Post Return under two former Fort Reid officers, William M. Fulton and Ephraim Thayer. McKissack and Hunter were other transfers to Fort Mellon, although Hunter and Fulton had been at Fort Mellon earlier.

Major Ashby also stated in January of 1841 that the garrison of Fort Reid was "reduced" by one company that had gone to Fort Mellon. The implication is that Fort Reid continued to function, although no more post returns were made. We do know that as of February 1 Colonel Twiggs was still being addressed by Surg. R. S. Satterlee as commander of the St. Johns District at Fort Reid. Satterlee had brought to the attention of Twiggs a serious health hazard prevalent at Fort Reid; Twiggs in turn wrote the adjutant general regarding 90 men on his sick list, 50 of whom could not possibly recover without a change of location and water. He further pointed out that during the life of the post the average monthly sick count had been 122, with 33 deaths and 19 discharges by surgeon's certificate of disability. (These figures exceed the number appearing as statistics in the appendix to Sprague's *Florida War.*) The dysentery and fever were attributed by Surgeon Satterlee to the "malarial influence," despite the fact that order 23 had admonished that "In selecting new positions regard must be had to the healthfulness of the site and to the facility of obtaining good water." Twiggs told the adjutant general that "humanity if not other feeling would dictate some place to save so many lives as are now in immediate danger" and recommended that a hospital be established on the "Sea Board" twenty-eight miles away.[9]

Another victim of this "sickly season" was the regimental music. Twiggs reported the "break up" of the band due to illness and requested permission to send Lieutenant Darling (listed in the November post return) to recruit musicians at New York. The request was granted.[10]

Major J. A. Ashby, the last commander of Fort Reid, also looked to New York for relief but for another reason. His rather terse letter to Colonel Twiggs from Fort Reid, dated January 8, 1841, reads as follows: "Having spent the summers of 1836, 1837, 1839 & 1840 in Florida, I am anxious to spend that of 1841 out of it. I therefore request that you will be pleased to have me detailed on the recruiting service in the city of New York." In adding his recommendation to this request Colonel Twiggs perhaps suggested a little sympathy for Ashby in saying upon Ashby's departure, "It is to be hoped that *some* of the Captains, who are now absent, may be induced to pay a visit to their Companies."[11] Such were the subjects during the closing months at Fort Reid, in addition to the problem of deserters, one of whom in a rage tore up a valuable set of music books and vowed never to play another note.[12]

The garrison at Fort Reid may have been transferred back to Fort Mellon in January 1841 for reasons other than the health of the men. General Armistead seems to have had second thoughts about Fort Mellon as the landing place for Fort Reid, and in a letter of June 2, 1840, only one month before the opening of Fort Reid, he made the following observation to the adjutant general: "Since the commencement of this War, this Chief [Coacoochee] has had his retreat near Fort Mellon, from whence he has conducted all his expeditions against the Inhabitants East of the St. Johns, but never while Fort Mellon was properly garrisoned."[13] After January 1841 Fort Reid apparently served as a blockhouse for civilian defense rather than as a staging area for a planned military campaign. It has been said that there was a blockhouse in the 2400 block on the west side of Mellonville Avenue and that earthworks were located at the 2000 block, also on the west side of Mellonville Avenue. The same source states that signals were exchanged between Fort Reid and Fort Mellon in the last stages of the Third Seminole War, which ended in 1858.[14] A further hint that Fort Reid limped along into this third stage of the war is given by a note in the lone October 1849 Fort Gatlin Post Return: Lt. Lewis Owen was absent on special duty commanding "Depot Guard at Ft. Reid E. Dist. Palatka." The command post of the St. Johns District eight years previously, Fort Reid had become just a depot in another district.

By 1882 the area around Fort Reid was being described as an "attractive little village" where were located some of the oldest, best, and most productive orange groves in the state. In 1903, the fort area was said to be located "near lake Monroe, in Orange County; now town of that name."[15] The trend away from Fort Mellon to Fort Reid continued over the years until finally the latter became a village, a suburb-in-waiting for Sanford.

Another area waiting for Sanford was Mellonville. As Fort Mellon grew less important after the war, the village of Mellonville emerged in its shadow. The pier that Peyton and Davidson had crudely shown as an appendage to the fort continued to serve as a steamboat terminus; the fort with its seven or eight buildings became the nucleus of a town from where overland travel began. When in 1845 a new seat for the newly named Orange County was sought, Mellonville (spelled Mellonsville in the enabling act) was selected in place of Enterprise, where the previous county seat had been. Enterprise, first settled in 1841 by Maj. Cornelius Taylor, a cousin of Zachary Taylor, had been troubled by typhoid fever, which had claimed the life of Cornelius Taylor's thirteen-year-old daughter, Polly. (Her gravestone still stands in Enterprise, on the property of H. C. Cobb.) Taylor left Enterprise in 1837, probably because of his daughter's death and because of the paucity of other settlers.[16] In 1845 Mellonville with its steamboat pier and fort buildings doubtless presented itself as the most advantageous site for the county seat created by the first session of the newly established state legislature. One of the fort's government buildings was used as the office of the newly appointed Orange County clerk of the court, Arthur Ginn.[17]

Mellonville continued as the seat of Orange County until Orlando succeeded it in 1856. Some confusion on this point exists due to the statement in Blackman's *History of Orange County* (page 31) that "The county seat of Orange County, which had previously been at Enterprise, was removed to Orlando in 1856." On the following page, however, a quotation from the first extant entry (April 20, 1847) of the Orange County Court contains the phrase "at the court house in Mellonville"; a second quotation (page 33) refers to Mellonville in 1849 as "the Seat of Justice." To clarify the somewhat confusing sequence of events — new state, new counties, and new county seats — I give the following chronology:

February 24, 1843 The governor and council of the territory of Florida named Enterprise the county seat of Mosquito County.

January 30, 1845 The same governor and council changed the name of Mosquito County to Orange County.

March 3, 1845 Florida was admitted as a state.

July 16, 1845 The first Florida State Legislature moved the county seat of Orange County from Enterprise to Mellonville.

December 22, 1845 Volusia County was created, and Enterprise was made the county seat.

December 30, 1856 The county seat of Orange County was moved from Mellonville to Orlando.

December 30, 1888 The county seat of Volusia County was moved from Enterprise to DeLand.[18]

It is interesting to note that Enterprise, Sanford's neighbor across the lake, has been the seat of three counties: of Mosquito for about two years, of Orange County for about six months, and of Volusia County for thirty-four years. Sanford has been (as Mellonville) the seat of Orange County and, since 1913, the seat of Seminole County.

In 1860 Mellonville was the only post office for a large area of Orange County; it was also a center for cotton grown around Apopka and shipped to Savannah and Charleston. Landing at Doyle's Dock at Mellonville, boat passengers found their way southwest through the woods to newer settlements forming in Orange

County. By 1866 the government fort buildings had been removed, and Mellonville, with one large emporium and one house, became the trading center for a broad area. In 1871 the Mellonville school enrollment of fifty was the largest in the county — Orlando could boast only thirty, Apopka only twenty-five. Mellonville in 1873 had two general stores, a so-called hotel, a saloon, and two cottages. In 1874 an Orlando public notice referred to the *Mellonville Advertiser,* which indicates the existence of a newspaper.[19]

Although Mellonville was incorporated in the 1870s, it began to lose out to Sanford, its newer and more prosperous neighbor, which was incorporated in 1877. George M. Barbour may have precipitated the state's action in officially dissolving Mellonville in 1883 the following year, for in 1882 he reported that "one mile east of Sanford is Mellonville, merely a pier, and old hotel, and a few dwellings. . . the landing for the town and garrison of Fort Reed, 2 miles in the interior."[20] During the period after the Seminole War people were also settling in the Fort Reid area, away from Fort Mellon.

It might be helpful to recapitulate the Fort Mellon satellite forts by indicating their respective positions and sponsors: Fort Lane was created by Jesup as the first stepping stone from Fort Mellon following the course of the upper St. Johns south to its headwaters, where he ultimately encountered the Seminoles at Okeechobee. Fort Kingsbury appears to have been merely a temporary camp adjunct of Fort Mellon. In November of 1838 General Taylor felt it necessary to consolidate after the battles of the Loxahatchee and Okeechobee and to protect the citizens against the Seminoles by creating a strong line of defense running from New Smyrna to Tampa. Along this line were to be strong posts every twenty miles,[21] which explains forts Maitland and Gatlin. Fort Reid, the last of the forts spun off from Fort Mellon, was established in 1840 by General Armistead as described in this chapter.

Chapter 10
The Fort Mellon Roster

I have mentioned all; it is because all deserve mention.
Col. A. C. W. Fanning, February 9, 1837

The roster now included the names of several who were not unknown to fame or were destined to make their mark in the future.
T. F. Rodenbough, 1875

There are three listings of personnel pertinent to Fort Mellon. One is the list of officers who took part in the battle of Camp Monroe and of whom Fanning made favorable mention in his report. The second list comprises the officers of the Second Dragoons and includes six whose names became part of the local geography. The third list derives from the Fort Mellon post returns, from which in turn I have made a secondary list of West Point graduates. The relevant names in these lists, plus the three generals, the diarist, and the two mapmakers of Fort Mellon, represent the unofficial Fort Mellon roster.

Colonel Fanning's Roster

CAPT. CHARLES MELLON

Not much is known about Charles Mellon of the Second Regiment of Artillery. According to Fanning, the two of them entered the army in 1812; in 1814 Mellon wrote from Bellefonte (Pennsylvania) to Secretary of War Armstrong accepting his appointment as an officer. His letter reads:

> This moment I received the appointment of third Lieutenant in the first regiment of Artillery, dated the 17th ultimo, which you did me the honor to send — I cheerfully accept of the appointment and shall by the first mail report myself to Captain Reed according to

orders, and shall hold myself ready at a moments warning to receive and obey further orders —

Please to accept my cordial thanks for the distinguished favor you have confered on me to deserve which shall be the study of my life which I hereby devote to the service of my country.[1]

The Military Service Records of the National Archives (GSA) contain no biographical information on Mellon. He first comes to our attention in Florida at Fort King (Ocala), where in November of 1835 he, now a captain, was in command of Company F, Second Artillery. On December 31 he was in action at the first battle of the Withlacoochee, where he is said to have exhibited great bravery and judgment — he offered to swim the river to obtain a canoe, and he was the first to fire at a stalking Indian. When the Indians threatened the right flank, Captain Mellon and another officer drove them off with a bayonet attack. He returned home in June 1836, was back again in January of 1837, and the next month was killed in the battle of Camp Monroe.[2]

Motte defined Mellon's grave as being in an angle of the fort breastwork. Another source describes the grave thus: "A little rectangular colonade of palmetto pickets enclose it. Over his grave is placed a broad tablet, of that rare and peculiar stone... and on it is chiselled the name and rank of the departed, with a notice of the manner and occasion of his death." Sprague in 1839 said that "His grave is enclosed with pickets and covered with a stone slab without any inscription."[3]

In the appendix to his *Florida War* Sprague cites an army order (July 25, 1842) to gather the remains of all fatalities of the Second Seminole War for interment on August 15, 1842, at what was then called St. Francis Barracks in St. Augustine, where a monument was erected. The Saint Augustine Historical Society advises that

> there is no record to show that Charles Mellon or Charles Kings- bury were buried at St. Francis Barracks, now the National Ceme- tery. However, a letter to the Assistant Adjutant General from Brevet Brigadier-General R. H. Jackson dated St. Augustine, Fla., September 14, 1881 states, "From all the information obtainable at this place it is supposed that all the officers and soldiers who died in the territory of Florida, or were killed in battle during the Florida War, are buried in this cemetery."

The same letter later states, "It is a pity that no records of the graves marked on the 'plat' and numbered XIX to LXVII, inclusive, can be

Bellefonte April 9th 1814

Sir,

This moment I received the appointment of third Lieutenant in the first regiment of Artillery dated the 17th ultimo which you did me the honor to send — I chearfully accept of the appointment and shall by the first Mail report myself to Captain Reed according to orders, and shall hold myself ready at a moments warning to receive and obey further orders. Please to accept my cordial thanks for the distinguished favor you have conferred on me to deserve which shall be my the study of my life which I hereby devote to the service of my country

I am Sir your most Obedient Servant

Charles Mellon

The Honorable John Armstrong
Secretary of war

The manuscript of Capt. Charles Mellon's letter to Secretary of War John Armstrong, April 9, 1814, accepting his commission. (National Archives)

85

found at the post." Sprague also notes that on the south face of the monument is inscribed, "A minute record of all the officers who perished and are here or elsewhere deposited, as also a portion of the soldiers." Thus no records attest to the reinterment of Mellon's remains at St. Augustine, and given the disappearance of Fort Mellon by 1866 and the later changes in the Sanford waterfront, there is little hope of ever knowing the final resting place. J. N. Whitner recorded that Mellon and other soldiers who died at the fort were interred on the land adjacent to the southeast wing of the Mayfair Hotel (until recently the Sanford Naval Academy) and that several older townspeople recalled having visited the graves, which were so near the water's edge that all traces have long been washed away.[4]

Both Dr. Alfred J. Hanna of Rollins College and T. A. Mellon were speakers at the Founders Day celebration in Sanford on February 8, 1937, one hundred years after Capt. Charles Mellon's death. In his speech T. A. Mellon (the nephew of Andrew W. Mellon, secretary of the Treasury in the Harding, Coolidge, and Hoover cabinets) explained his interest in the subject and previewed his monograph on Charles Mellon that appeared in the *Florida Historical Quarterly* later in the year; he said that his own connection with Captain Mellon was rather remote, their common ancestor of Scottish origin having later settled in county Tyrone (Ireland).

It is thought that the Charles Mellon family emigrated from Ireland before the Andrew Mellon branch of the family did the same.[5] Charles Mellon himself settled and lived in Pennsylvania, but the exact time and place is not certain. His letter of April 9, 1814, to the secretary of war from Bellefonte might indicate that as his home; however, inquiry to Centre County produced no evidence of Charles Mellon or a Mellon family. Other evidence points to Erie (Pennsylvania). In his report on the battle Fanning noted the inadequacy of Mellon's pension (twenty-five dollars per month for five years) to his widow and four children. On March 30, 1848, six years after the pension had expired, Report 447 was presented to the House of Representatives by its Committee on Invalid Pensions; it pointed out that Mellon's widow Eliza, resident of Erie for several years, was destitute with a family of five, one a permanent invalid girl. The report further stated that the original pension had expired in 1842 and had never been renewed. A bill was proposed for the relief of Eliza A. Mellon at the rate of twenty dollars per month, to begin February 8, 1847, and to continue for her natural life; however, it is not known whether this bill was ever passed.[6] Questioning of the historical societies of Erie and Crawford County revealed no evidence of a Mellon family in the Erie area. So both Mellon's home and his final resting place remain in question.

Charles Mellon's name is pre-
served today by Mellonville Avenue and Fort Mellon Park in Sanford.
The name of Capt. William Maitland, by contrast, is preserved in the
town of Maitland and in Lake Maitland, neither of which he ever saw. At
least Captain Mellon did see Camp Monroe, to which his name was later
given.

LT. GEORGE CUMMINS THOMAS

Second Lieutenant George C. Thomas (1812-82) from New Jersey and of
the Fourth Artillery was the officer Colonel Fanning directed to board
the steamboat *Santee,* to "serve the six pounder, and direct his fire upon
the right of the enemy." His second tour of duty at Fort Mellon is recorded
by Pickell on November 16 when his name was included with the other
officers of Pickell's Fourth Artillery leaving Black Creek for Fort Mellon,
as well as in the November post returns.

Thomas was a cadet at the United
States Military Academy from July 1, 1832, to July 1, 1836, after which
he was breveted a second lieutenant in the Fourth Artillery. In this
capacity, apart from his role in the defense of Camp Monroe, he served in
operations against the Creeks and during the removal of the Cherokees
in 1838. As a first lieutenant he saw action on the northern frontier in
Michigan during Canadian border disturbances and was stationed at Fort
Mackinac up to 1841. He resigned in 1842. During the Civil War
Thomas was in command of the volunteers and militia of the District of
Columbia; later, until he retired in 1882, he was a civil employee in the
War Department. He should not be confused with George Henry
Thomas, who also served in the Seminole War and who later in the Civil
War became famous as the "Rock of Chickamauga."

The only other Florida battle ac-
tion involving George Cummins Thomas was at Fort Lauderdale in 1841,
when he accompanied a twelve-canoe expedition inland in pursuit of
Indians. I have already quoted Motte's description of Thomas' horseback
episode with Lieutenant McLaughlin two nights before the battle of
Camp Monroe.[7]

It is believed that the muzzle of
the *Santee's* six-pounder that Thomas fired during the battle of Camp
Monroe now serves as the base for the flagpole in front of the Sanford
Chamber of Commerce building. If so, it might deserve a more worthy
means of display.

LT. JOHN T. McLAUGHLIN

Navy Lieutenant McLaughlin, whom Fanning refers to as "Passed-Midshipman," was at the time of the battle serving as Fanning's adjutant. Like Mellon he received a ball in his breast; his wound was not fatal but did incapacitate him for nineteen months. Motte notes that he returned to Florida on November 29, 1838. Motte and McLaughlin were associated in an amphibious operation down Indian River below New Smyrna; McLaughlin's fleet then consisted of about a dozen Mackinaw boats, and his flagship was a fast-sailing sloop. As commander of the Florida Expedition (sometimes called the Florida Squadron) he had a force of 140 dugout canoes and about 10 schooners and barges manned by over four hundred men. With a flotilla of dugouts he led the first party of white men ever to cross the full width of the Everglades. In 1840 it was Lieutenant McLaughlin who transferred the body of Dr. Henry Perrine from his schooner *Flirt* to the *Santee*.[8]

CAPT. JOHN ROGERS VINTON

Born in Rhode Island, Captain Vinton of the Third Artillery graduated from West Point (1817) in 2½ years; and as Fanning pointed out, he added Captain Mellon's company to his own after the latter's fall. The post returns for March and April 1837 indicate that he was second in command at Fort Mellon for these months; in April he was assigned by Jesup's order 79 to notify the owners of runaway slaves to claim their property at St. Marks. Later in the year, Jesup sent Vinton to Washington as his special messenger on the subject of the Cherokee Deputation. In Jesup's November 10 letter to Poinsett, Vinton is described as one "who from his long service here, his knowledge of the Indians and the country, and his general intelligence, will be able to give full information on all matters connected with the subject of the war, and the views and conditions of the Indians."[9] In fact, Vinton was generally considered one of the most talented, accomplished, and effective officers in the service.

Prior to his appearance at Camp Monroe, Vinton had served at various garrisons and on special assignments, on a boundary survey, as an aide-de-camp, and in the Adjutant General's Office in Washington. Assistant Surgeon Forry, writing from Fort Taylor in 1838, describes another aspect of Vinton's character: the captain and the Reverend Bvt. Maj. John L. Gardner presented a dovetailed sermon on Sundays to a congregation of officers, soldiers, and two black guides. The two officers also conducted a Bible class every evening. Gardner was the commander of Fort Mellon between December 1838 and February 1839 as can be seen from the post returns.

Vinton subsequently led an expedition across the Everglades into the Big Cypress in 1842. Later he fought in the Mexican War and was lost by the blast of a shell at the siege of Vera Cruz, March 22, 1847. Fort Vinton, named after him, was eighteen miles northwest of Indian River Inlet.[10]

COL. ALEXANDER CAMPBELL WILDER FANNING

Colonel Fanning (1788-1846) is pictured as a diminutive figure and an energetic officer who had lost one arm by the accidental discharge of a musket while mustering on the Boston Common in 1808. The son of Capt. Barclay Fanning, who served in the British army during the American Revolution, he graduated from West Point in 1812 and first distinguished himself in the War of 1812 at the capture of York, Ontario, where he was severaly wounded — subsequently he was breveted from first lieutenant to major. He began his twenty-one year Florida military career with Andrew Jackson in 1818, at which time he was a member of the court martial and acted as provost marshal at the execution of the Englishmen Armbrister and Arbuthnot. In 1835 he was breveted to a colonel for his conduct in the first battle of the Withlacoochee.

Fanning seems to have attempted to compensate for his small stature and handicap by immersing himself in the military. He was one of the signers to a Seminole agreement in 1835; he commanded Fort St. Marks, Fort Gadsden, and Fort King and at the latter clapped Osceola in chains; he opened Camp Monroe and named Fort Mellon; and he built Fort Maitland. The little officer was also articulate. Bemrose said of him that he "never commanded his troops when in the woods but he by every action told you it was war. His word of command spoke of battle, his voice was so earnestly thrilling that it went through me. . . his own peculiar shrill ring of voice that went through you with its decisional energy." He did not hesitate to offer advice in strategy during battle, and he also expressed himself on overall war policy. We may note his resourcefulness at the battle of Camp Monroe, his analysis of individual performance after the affair, and his forthright unilateral decision to assign Fort Mellon its name. If Bemrose is correct, Fanning was treacherously murdered as a prisoner of war in Mexico; however, Cullum records that Fanning died in Cincinnati in 1846.[11]

The Second Dragoon Roster

The roster of the Second Dragoons includes personnel pertinent to Fort Mellon: four companies of the Second Dragoons were stationed at the fort, and the commandant for most of 1837 was Major Harney, the second ranking officer of the Dragoons. After the battle of Camp Monroe Fanning praised the valor of the dragoons and specifically mentioned ten of its officers as worthy of praise.

The Second Dragoons was created by presidential act, due to the need for Indian fighting in Florida and elsewhere. It was a mounted force and after 1875 was assimilated into the cavalry. The name comes from France, where the word dragon was first applied to a pistol hammer, so named because of its shape, then to the firearm, and then to the troops so armed.

The colored emblematic frontispiece to Rodenbough's *From Everglade to Canyon* presents a picture history of the Second Dragoons. The banners on the emblem bear the dates 1836 and 1875, representing the Second Dragoons' baptism in Florida and its 1875 termination in Montana. In the upper left corner a shield, one of five, shows the name "Florida" (campaign) and the dates 1836 and 1842, representing six years in Florida. Specific names of campaigns arranged in a semicircle across the top begin with "Micanopy" (the dragoons' introduction to Florida in 1836), and continue with "Fort Mellon."[12]

Listed below are the Second Dragoon officer staff appointments made pursuant to the presidential act and the assignment of officers made by Colonel Twiggs:

COLONEL
David E. Twiggs

MAJORS
William S. Harney
Thomas T. Fauntleroy

CAPTAINS
William Gordon
John Dougherty
John F. Lane
James A. Ashby
Jonathan L. Bean
Stinson H. Anderson
William W. Tompkins
Henry W. Fowler
Benjamin L. Beall
Edward S. Winder

FIRST LIEUTENANTS
Thornton Grimsley
Theophilus Holmes
Horatio Grooms
Thomas S. Bryant
John Graham
Townshend Dade
Erasmus D. Bullock
Marshall S. Howe
Charles Spalding
James W. Hamilton

SECOND LIEUTENANTS
William Gilpin
William H. Ward
George Forsyth
Croghan Ker
John H. P. O'Neale
John W. S. McNeil
Zebulon M. P. Maury
Seth Thornton
Charles E. Kingsbury
Charles A. May

In compliance with the instructions from the War Department, Colonel Twiggs made the following assignment of officers (Holmes had resigned and been replaced by Blake):

COMPANIES	CAPTAINS	FIRST LIEUTENANTS	SECOND LIEUTENANTS
A	Gordon	Grimsley	Ward
B	Dougherty	Grooms	Ker
C	Lane	Graham	Maury
D	Ashby	Spalding	Thornton
E	Bean	Hamilton	Gilpin
F	Anderson	Howe	McNeil
G	Tompkins	Blake	O' Neale
H	Fowler	Dade	May
I	Beall	Bullock	Forsyth
K	Winder	Bryant	Kingsbury

COL. WILLIAM SELBY HARNEY

The son of a major in the Revolution, Harney (1800-89) was born in Tennessee near the home of Andrew Jackson. His infantry commission in 1818 was handed to him by General Jesup. Harney had seen nearly twenty years service, part of it in the Black Hawk War under Zachary Taylor, before joining the Second Dragoons as second commanding officer in 1836, first with the rank of major, two months later raised to lieutenant colonel at President Andrew Jackson's Hermitage. Besides commanding Fort Mellon, he was the dragoon officer in charge at the battles of Camp Monroe and the Loxahatchee and on the expedition into the Everglades in the Seminole War. In 1840 he established Fort Reid from which post he commanded the district south of New Smyrna.

He also was in command of four battles in the Mexican War and served in the Sioux Expedition of 1855-56. He retired in 1863 and was breveted a major general in 1865.

Harney was commandant of Fort Mellon for about five months in 1837, the most active and sensitive time in the history of the fort. This period demanded close attention to the interplay of Indian, army, and government relations. Harney controlled about twenty-five hundred Indians encamped around the fort during the Capitulation by doling out rations, attending a lacrosse game, and giving Osceola the hospitality of his tent; but he was also required to be firm with the Indians, especially in carrying out some of Jesup's harsh orders.

Standing six feet three inches and with a thatch of red hair Harney has been described as having a fine physical and soldierly appearance and as being an experienced fighter and a good judge of men and horses. During his career in Florida he had several narrow escapes in Indian encounters. It is said that he could command by his mere presence but that he was somewhat of a bully, especially where "inferior" races were concerned. Of his conduct during the battle of Camp Monroe, Colonel Fanning said that Harney displayed "the greatest boldness and vigour, — and inspired his newly enlisted men with great confidence." Because of his involvement with exploration in connection with the Davidson map, Lake Harney was named for him; yet he also left his name on a lake and valley in Oregon.

The regard in which Harney's peers held him can be judged by the central position given to his photograph in the dragoon emblematic chromo lithograph emblazonment. This later-life picture of him with white sideburns, moustache, and receding hairline is encircled by pictures of seven subsequent officers. The prominent display of his portrait suggests that Harney best exemplified the Second Dragoons' motto of *Per Aspera ad Astra* ("through difficulties to the stars").[13]

CAPT. JOHN F. LANE

Lane (1810-36), for whom Fort Lane was named, was born in Kentucky, graduated from the U.S. Military Academy in 1828, and was made a second lieutenant of the Fourth Artillery. His first assignment (1828-29) was as an assistant professor at West Point, first in mathematics, then in natural and experimental philosophy. From 1832 to 1834 he was occupied in transferring Indians west, and in 1835 he was in the Quartermaster General's Office in Washington. On March 14, 1836, he was made colonel of the Creek Indian regiment of 750 friendly Indians, who wore white turbans in battle to distinguish them from the enemy. On June 8 he became a captain of the Second Dragoons, but his first duty was short, as aide-de-camp to General Jesup from June 10 to July 24.

Lane's career came to an abrupt and untimely end at the age of twenty-six when on October 20, 1836, he ran a sword through his head. He may have been deranged by fever and fatigue, or it may have been an accident; one possible reason for suicide was his flogging (1836) of Representative John Ewing of Indiana on the streets of Washington, by which compulsive action he had first attracted the attention of Andrew Jackson. On the other hand, Lane could have taken pride in the invention of an India-rubber pontoon that was used for bridge building during the war or in his tour of duty as assistant engineer at the Delaware Breakwater project.[14]

CAPT. JAMES A. ASHBY

Born in New York State, James Ashby first comes to our attention in 1836 as a captain in Brisbane's Regiment of the Left Wing of General Eustis as part of Gen. Winfield Scott's campaign of the three wings. Later in the same year he began his dragoon career when he was designated as a captain by a general order of the adjutant general in the initial organization of the newly created Second Dragoons. In October he was promoted to major for gallantry and good conduct in the affair at Welika, in which he commanded and was severely wounded. During the Florida war he commanded the first company of Second Dragoons in the field.

To Captain Ashby fell the rather undesirable assignment under the general orders of Jesup and under the immediate command of General Hernandez on October 21, 1837, to capture Osceola under a white flag of truce. The order was carried out near Fort Peyton, and the captured included not only Osceola but also Coa Hadjo and about seventy others. In 1840 Captain Ashby was asked by General Taylor to proceed from Fort Kingsbury to Fort Pierce; in November 1840 and January 1841 he was in command of Fort Reid. Ashby resigned in 1841 and died in 1846. Lake Ashby on SR 415 between Osteen and Samsula was almost certainly named after him, as the lake was already so labeled in 1839 on army map L247-4.[15]

The emblazonment of the Second Dragoons, showing their Fort Mellon campaign. (*T. F. Rodenbough*, From Everglade to Canyon with the Second Dragoons, *frontispiece*)

CAPT. EDWARD S. WINDER

Winder, from Maryland, entered army service as a captain in the Second Dragoons on June 8, 1836. He served with credit in the Florida war and died on the Eastern shore of Maryland on March 7, 1849, of disease contracted in service. There is hardly a doubt that Lake Winder was named after him — this lake in Brevard County is one of the eight through which the St. Johns passes. Fort Taylor was located nearby.[16]

LT. JOHN WINFIELD SCOTT McNEIL

McNeil (1818-37) was the son of Brig. Gen. John McNeil and grandson of Gen. Benjamin Pierce, hero of the Revolution from New Hampshire and twice governor of that state. Franklin Pierce, the fourteenth president of the United States, was his uncle. The young lieutenant's middle names were no doubt given to him because of family military association. He was also on the Fanning merit list.

On September 7, 1837, near the blackened ruins of Dunlawton sugar mill, McNeil headed a company of fifty men under Lieutenant Peyton, the Lake Jessup cartographer. Having captured Emathla, McNeil's men were being led by an Indian prisoner guide, Tomoka John, in search of Yuchi Billy (shown on Peyton's map as Euchee Billy), whom they also captured, but only after McNeil had been mortally wounded. McNeil was the first and at nineteen years of age the youngest dragoon officer to die in the war. He had been a cadet at West Point from June 6, 1834, to January 1835 but left for service before graduating. Fort McNeil on Chickasaw Hatchee in Orange County, near Lake Poinsett, was named for him.[17]

LT. CHARLES E. KINGSBURY

Second Lieutenant Kingsbury has been mentioned in chapter 4 along with Motte's report that the lieutenant was buried at Fort Mellon. Kingsbury was one of the ten officers under Harney who received Fanning's praise. Apart from the March, April, and May 1837 post returns for Fort Mellon army records show only that he joined the Second Dragoons, along with Lane, Ashby, McNeil, and Winder, on June 8,

1836, as a second lieutenant. His military career, like McNeil's, was short and tragic; and like McNeil he had a fort named after him.[18]

LT. JOHN GRAHAM

John Graham (1814-41) from Pennsylvania entered the United States Military Academy at the age of fifteen in 1829 and graduated in 1834; during 1834-35 he served as a second lieutenant in the garrison at Fort King. Graham and Osceola were inseparable and were seen together daily; Lieutenant Cohen attributes their friendship to Graham's interest in Osceola's little daughter and in teaching Osceola to speak English. Consequently Osceola had given orders that Graham was to be spared in combat. Graham saw action in the battles of the Withlacoochee, Camp Monroe (Fort Mellon), Mosquito Inlet, and the Loxahatchee. On June 11, 1836, he joined the Second Dragoons, becoming a captain on October 1, 1837, in which year he was also for a short time aide-de-camp to General Hernandez. The Fort Mellon post returns indicate his presence during March, April, May, and November 1837. In 1838 he resigned but remained in Florida. On January 4, 1840, he became adjutant general of the territory of Florida, in which capacity he died at his plantation, Blackwood (seven miles north of Tallahassee), on July 30, 1841, in the same month as his father-in-law, Governor Robert Reid.[19]

Concerning seven more on the dragoon and Fort Mellon post return rosters, an interesting story of their fast overland equestrian trip from St. Louis appears in the *Jacksonville Courier* in 1837:

The following is a list of officers belonging to a detachment (Companies A, B, C, and K) of the Second Dragoons, arrived in camp about a mile from our town, October 31:

Colonel D. E. Twiggs, commanding; Captains W. W. Tompkins, E. S. Winder, W. M. Fulton, and L. J. Beall; Lieutenants E. D. Bullock, A. A. Q. M., R. B. Lawton, and L. Darling, Acting Adjutant.

We were surprised to witness the fresh and healthy appearance of this body of officers and men after so long and, at times, difficult march. The condition of the horses, at the same time, struck us forcibly as evidencing a high state of order and attention. The detachment left Jefferson Barracks, Missouri, September 5, and marched through Illinois to Shawneetown, crossing the Ohio; thence through a portion of Kentucky to Nashville, Tennessee; thence over the Cumberland Mountains, crossed the Tennessee River to the Lookout Mountain at Ross's Landing; thence to this place, *marching, from an actual calculation, twelve hundred miles in fifty five days.*[20]

Of the officers mentioned above, only Twiggs and Beall established military careers. Winder died in 1849; the other five all resigned between 1841 and 1848. Beall resigned in 1861, and Twiggs, born in 1790, ended his career in 1861 as a major general in the Confederate army.

With regard to the initial dragoon staff, one third resigned before 1841, about another third went on into the Mexican War, and the balance either died or were killed early. Four had declined their original appointments. Lieutenant George Alexander Hamilton Blake, one of the ten dragoon officers praised by Fanning, is the only officer of the Camp Monroe battle to take part in all subsequent campaigns up to and including Gettysburg. After the Mexican War he served in Missouri, Texas, New Mexico, Arizona, California, Nevada, Oregon, and Washington. He retired in 1870 as a major general and died in 1884. Harney retired as a major general in 1863; he did not participate in the Civil War.[21]

In 1837 General Clinch rather belatedly included three officers of our roster, Fanning, Mellon, and Graham, in a letter recommending them to the particular notice of the president of the United States for their conduct at the battle of the Withlacoochee, December 31, 1835.[22] In House of Representatives Document 219 (March 12, 1838), which is essentially a report of the battle of the Loxahatchee, the staff officers Jesup, Eustis, Twiggs, Harney, Gates, and Bankhead singled out as worthy of special mention the following former or later Fort Mellon officers: Pickell, Washington, Davidson, Anderson, Tompkins, and May.

The Fort Mellon Mapmakers and Diarist

LT. RICHARD A. PEYTON

Peyton (1811-39), who drew the Fort Mellon map of Lake Jessup, was from Virginia and attended the military academy from 1827 to 1831. At graduation he was made a first lieutenant. From 1832 to 1834 he served at West Point as assistant professor of mathematics; in 1836-37 he was participating in operations against the Creeks. The post returns show that he was at Fort Mellon between March and May 1837. Davidson writes that Peyton discovered Lake Jessup on May 22; Motte relates that he met Peyton at Fort Mellon on June 11.

In September Peyton was in command of his own post, Fort Peyton, seven miles south of St. Augustine. Under orders of General Hernandez he made the capture of Yuchi Billy, during which encounter Lieutenant McNeil was killed. During 1838 Peyton served as chief of commissary in the emigration of the Cherokee Indians to the west of the Mississippi. He died in 1839 at the age of twenty-eight while assistant quartermaster at Fort Brooke, Tampa Bay.[23]

LT. WILLIAM B. DAVIDSON

Lieutenant Davidson, who made the Fort Mellon map of the Lake Harney expedition on November 10, 1837, was from Virginia and an 1815 West Point graduate. He was the lieutenant of the Third Artillery unit to whom Fanning delegated command of the Second Artillery at the fall of Mellon; of the exchange of command Fanning said, "It could not have fallen into better hands." After graduation, Davidson served in ordnance from 1815 to 1821 in garrisons at Fort Preble (Maine), Fort Severn (Maryland), and Fort Monroe (Virginia). As a first lieutenant in the Third Artillery he served in Washington in the Adjutant General's Office from 1825 to 1834. The Fort Mellon post returns list him during March, April, and May 1837. In December 1840 Davidson died on an expedition into the Everglades under Colonel Harney. His map is discussed in chapter 5.[24]

LT. JOHN PICKELL

Pennsylvania born, John Pickell (1802-65) was a cadet at the military academy from 1818 to 1822. Assigned to the Fourth Artillery after graduation, he served first in ordnance duty and then on topographical

98

duty for four years. In 1832 he was connected with the Black Hawk Expedition, and he was at Charleston harbor during the South Carolina threat of nullification. From 1833 to 1835 he was on engineer duty on the Cumberland Road. During 1836-38, as adjutant of the Fourth Artillery apart from his stay at Fort Mellon, he saw duty in the action at Fort Drane and the Loxahatchee. He resigned in 1838 after helping in the transfer of the Cherokees to the west that year. Needless to say, we are indebted to him for his daily record of events during his stay at Fort Mellon.

Later, in private life, Pickell was a civil engineer in Maryland (1839-41). From 1842 to 1843 he served as a member of the Maryland House of Representatives. While serving in the Maryland militia as a captain and a colonel (1844-50) he was also a director of the Chesapeake and Ohio Canal and a coal merchant in Baltimore. He was president of the National Fire Insurance Company of Baltimore in 1853 and of the Pickell Coal and Iron Company from 1855 to 1858. From 1859 to 1861 he was editor of the *Frostburg Gazette* and *Miners Records*.

During the Civil War, as colonel of the Thirteenth New York Volunteers, he commanded a regiment in the defense of Washington from 1861 to 1862, after which he resigned because of illness. He died in 1865 at Danville, New York.

An interesting aftermath of his Fort Mellon service in 1837 was a two-page letter Pickell wrote (January 16, 1844) to the adjutant general of the army in Washington on the subject of two saline rivulets falling into Lake Harney on its southern side, which he had noticed on his exploration detail under Colonel Bankhead. He described the rivulets as having a rapid current and an aggregate fall of several feet within a few yards of the shore and running into the lake from two to three miles southwest of the river. These rivulets, about eighteen inches wide by six inches in depth he judged, were formed by springs about two hundred yards from the shore. Upon tasting the water he found it more strongly impregnated with salt than was the water near Salinia and Syracuse, New York, where salt was manufactured commercially.

A letter dated February 23, 1844, from the commissioner, General Land Office, to the surveyor general, Tallahassee, that enclosed a copy of John Pickell's letter seems to have been the only official response. The commissioner commented that it would be expedient to alert the deputy to the report when the contract was given out for surveying the pertinent area. He further pointed out that to note the rivulets on the township plats would probably cause a much higher price for the adjacent land than if their existence were not indicated. On the same letter is a note admonishing that the "Deputy residing in the neighborhood of this land, to whom you could entrust the location of the claim, it would be expedient to employ him in order that the parties may not be put to any needless expense." From this it appears that Pickell was making a claim for the springs, but what was the outcome we do not know. He seems to have been overly optimistic about the presence of salt, which still can be obtained in the water of shallow wells but not in commercially significant amounts.[25]

The following list shows that over the five years of Fort Mellon's official reporting tenure some fifty-nine (including the five at Fort Reid) graduates or cadets from the U.S. Military Academy were stationed in the two forts whose sites are now embraced by Sanford. Besides being of local interest, this fact reflects the tremendous effort expended by our country in pursuing the Second Seminole War. The names are given by year of graduation.[26]

1806 Col. William Gates

1812 Col. Alexander C. W. Fanning

1815 Lt. William B. Davidson

1817 Capt. John Rogers Vinton
     Capt. John Marshall Washington

1818 Capt. Harvey Brown

1820 Lt. Samuel B. Dusenberry

1821 Lt. Edward C. Ross

1822 *Capt. Jonathan L. Bean
     Lt. John Pickell

1823 *Lt. James W. Hamilton
     Lt. Frederick Searle

1826 Lt. Silas Casey
     Lt. Danforth H. Tufts

1827 *Lt. Marshall S. Howe

1828 Lt. Charles O. Collins

1829 Lt. Franklin Eyre Hunt

1830 Capt. Lloyd James Beall
     Capt. George Waynefleet Patten
     Lt. Robert H. Kirkwood Whitley

1831 Lt. Richard H. Peyton

1832 Lt. George Watson

1833 Lt. Isaac R. D. Burnett
     Lt. Nathaniel Wyche Hunter
     Lt. John Henry Miller
     Lt. Alexander Eakin Shiras

1834 Lt. William Grigsby Freeman
     Lt. John Graham

1835 Lt. Thomas Lee Brent
     Lt. Weightman Key Hanson
     Capt. William M. D. McKissack

1836 Lt. Robert Allen
     Lt. Robert Fulton Baker
     Lt. Samuel I. Bransford
     Lt. William Mock
     Lt. John Paul Jones O'Brien
     Lt. John Wolcott Phelps
     Lt. George Cummins Thomas
     Lt. Christopher Quarles Tompkins

1837 Lt. Edmund Bradford
   Lt. John Williams Gunnison
   Lt. Robert Tignall Jones
   Lt. William Thomas Martin
   Lt. John Clifford Pemberton
   Lt. Henry Clay Pratt
   Lt. James Russell Soley
   Lt. Edward Jenner Steptoe
   Lt. George Taylor
   Lt. Thomas Williams
   Lt. Francis Octavus Wyse

1838 Lt. Ripley Allen Arnold
   Lt. Zebulon Montgomery Pike Inge
   *Lt. John Winfield Scott McNeil
   Lt. Owen P. Ransom
   Lt. Henry Hopkins Sibley

1840 Lt. Reuben Philander Campbell
   Lt. Fowler Hamilton
   Lt. Thomas Lee Ringgold

*Left academy for service before graduation

There were in addition to the above fifty-nine approximately fifty-two other commissioned officers and surgeons who served at Fort Mellon and Fort Reid, including all the top generals and the three chief commanders of the dragoons. One of the surgeons, Samuel Preston Moore, who served five months at Fort Mellon and Fort Reid, went on to become surgeon general of the Confederacy from 1861 to 1865. (In this role he is one of the minor but historical characters in Frank Slaughter's *The Stonewall Brigade*.) Some of the most familiar and colorful names of American history appear as given names in this list: Henry Clay, Robert Fulton, Alexander Hamilton, John Paul Jones, John Marshall, Zebulon Montgomery Pike, and Winfield Scott. These names engender the feeling that the Fort Mellon story is a genuine part of American history.

The Fort Mellon Generals

GEN. THOMAS SIDNEY JESUP

Jesup (1788-1860) was the fourth general in charge of military operations in the Florida War. He succeeded Winfield Scott (Gen. Richard Keith Call had been in charge until Jesup arrived on December 8, 1836) and held command for eighteen months before yielding to Zachary Taylor, whose two-year term was the longest of the war.

A Virginian, Jesup entered the army in 1808, at twenty years of age, with a rank of second lieutenant and served in the War of 1812. By 1818 he was quartermaster general, which post he continued to hold for forty-two years until his death in 1860, a record term. President Madison showed high regard in sending Jesup to the 1818 Hartford convention in Connecticut to report any secession movement. Not much is known about the general apart from his activities in Florida, which made him a controversial figure and the most important white man in the Seminole War.

Jesup's most controversial action is referred to in Pickell's entry of November 30, which notes that Osceola was a captive in St. Augustine. In the words of Surgeon Motte, Osceola had announced at his camp under a white flag that he had thrown away his rifle and had brought only his ball (lacrosse) sticks for one or two days ball play after the talk. Jesup did not play ball either literally or figuratively. His seizure of Osceola under a flag of truce produced a popular reaction in the country something like the army's program of defoliation in the recent Vietnam War. In fairness to Jesup it should be pointed out that shortly after Osceola's incarceration, the general wrote to the War Department: "If I were permitted. . . I would allow them [the Seminoles] to remain, and would assign them to the country west of the Kissimmee, Okee-Chobee, and Panai-Okee, and east of Pease Creek, south to the extreme of Florida." Near the end of his career in Florida, he urged the War Department to accept a definite proposal of this nature having the backing of General Eustis and Colonel Twiggs. But while allowing himself these personal expressions of opinion, he was obligated to enforce the emigration policy. In view of his remark that "the difficulty is not to fight the enemy but to find him," it is understandable that to his way of thinking the quickest and least violent way to end the conflict was to seize Seminoles under any circumstances and force them into emigration. On the other hand, a much later unofficial army opinion on this matter has pointed out that "No excuse, however, should be offered for the abuse of the flag of truce, which was begun by a general officer and followed by several others."[27]

A point in Jesup's favor was his organizational ability in military planning. A very apt phrase used in describing his role in the Delaware Breakwater project of 1834 referred to Jesup's exercise of "surgically keen logic" in his analysis and rejection of a proposal. No other general in the Florida War approached him in this ability, which he no doubt owed to his long experience as quartermaster general. As pointed out previously he commanded in 1837 the largest number of troops ever assembled in Florida. The situation created by the slave article in the Capitulation required tact in reconciling political pressure with army duties. In short, the subjects with which Jesup had to deal ran the gamut: establishing upriver posts like Fort Mellon, exploring the upper St. Johns, capturing Seminole chiefs by methods he realized would be unpopular, solving the Indian-black aspect of the Capitulation to everyone's satisfaction, planning battles, fighting them with and against the Indians, overseeing the Cherokee Deputation — even checking the possibility of dredging to facilitate better steamboat channels in lakes George and Monroe. Jesup did capture the largest number of Seminoles with the largest army of the war. He did not succeed in terminating the conflict, but neither did any of his successors.[28]

BVT. BRIG. GEN. ABRAHAM EUSTIS

Prior to the Florida war, Eustis had been commanding at Charleston. I have noted that early in 1836 the citizens of Charleston drafted Eustis to supervise the organizing and sending of several companies of troops to Florida via the *John Stoney* and the *Santee*. In the same year the general commanded the left wing and made the longest and hardest march of Winfield Scott's campaign of the three wings.

Both Bemrose and Cohen, who served under Eustis, were critical of his personality but not his ability. Bemrose rather succinctly sums up the general impression Eustis seems to have made:

Gen. Eustis was a strict disciplinarian, just to all grades, volunteers or militia, all received from him their due and no more. Consequently he was not a favorite with many of the officers and he was positively hated by the proud volunteers. It is quite common for the commissioned privates to get extra attention from their commanders. It appears politic so to treat them.

The volunteers, both officers and privates, had by other generals received considerable attention, but Gen. Eustis would not descend to tact or any of these flatteries to gain a questionable good name. He was a thorough soldier, just to all but fearing none. He sought not to gain popularity, only by doing his duty and seeing that others did their duty. He therefore was fitted to command large armies but as he was upright and not politic he was as gall and wormwood to the proud southern volunteers. These certainly consisted of the elite of Georgia, South Carolina, Louisiana, and Florida. It was known that Gen. Shelton of the Carolina militia was a private, and many more such were content to serve in the campaign, laying aside their various grades, ranks, or station. Planters, merchants, and physicians all served as common soldiers and were generally treated by their officers with great consideration, but Gen. Eustis of the regular army could not be made to see or know any such distinction. If a gentleman came as a common soldier, he was treated by him fairly but not flattered and no liberties were allowed.

Cohen cites as evidence of Eustis' lack of communication with his troops his failure to show himself to them as their commander on any dress parade or other assemblage. In fact, Eustis avoided dress parades and appeared only in mufti, disdaining display of the sword or any other badge of office. Cohen sums up his general impression of Eustis:

His words are few, and as un-like a courtier's as roughness is to polish, or harshness to suavity. The jests of Gen. E. are still fewer, and are the most solemn, serious things in the world — they are any thing but laughing matter. His grace is *such* as oftener to throw sand between the helmet and the wound of the soldier, then to pour in the latter the wine and the oil of balmy consolation. Yet Gen. E is a brave commander, and a business man.

That he was a "thorough soldier" and "a brave commander" was also recognized by General Jesup, who put Eustis in charge of the St. Johns Wing, which took off from Fort Mellon and Fort Lane in December of 1837 and ultimately fought in the battle of the Loxahatchee. Pickell noted in his entry of December 13 that the command of General Hernandez had been placed under General Eustis. Leaving the Fort Mellon area on December 17, Eustis led his St. Johns Wing south, traveling west of the St. Johns. On December 25 he erected Fort Christmas; on January 16 he arrived at Fort Taylor, established 100 miles south of Fort Mellon by Colonel Twiggs, who had been sent in advance. Jesup did not expect that Eustis would travel more than 14 or 15 miles per day; in fact, Eustis encountered so much difficulty that he advanced less than 30 miles in three days. Motte states that Eustis had in reaching the head of the St. Johns, not far from the site of the recent battle of Okeechobee, "ac-complished a march of two hundred miles through the wilderness, in which they had to be constantly cutting roads through dismal swamps, and almost impenetrable hammocks, and bridging streams for the pas-sage of wagons; all the while exposed to the scorching beams of a tropical sun, or drenching torrents of rain." He had with him ten companies of the Third and Fourth Artillery and a large train of ambulances and baggage wagons. Eustis and his men were then only a few miles from the battle at the Loxahatchee, which was fought on January 24, 1838.

Jesup's respect for Eustis is evident

from his adoption of a suggestion made by Colonel Twiggs and Eustis after the battle of the Loxahatchee: that the war should be terminated by allowing the Indians to retain a small district in the south of the peninsula. Jesup adopted this as his own recommendation, but his superiors in Washington declined to agree; consequently, Jesup ordered Colonel Twiggs to seize the whole party of 513 Seminoles waiting for the reply from Washington, a move reminiscent of the earlier seizure of Osceola. Grabgame seems to be the term Captain Backus and others in the army applied to this tactic.

What Eustis thought of this conclusion to his suggestion can only be surmised. When General Scott left Florida in 1836, he temporarily turned over his command to Eustis as the next ranking officer in the field; it may be significant that Eustis accepted with the understanding that he wished to retain command no longer than necessary.

It is generally thought that the city of Eustis and its lake were named for Abraham Eustis. This is borne out by the fact that Lake Eustis was already so named on John Lee Williams' map of 1837 and on the 1823 map in Charles Vignoles' book.[29]

BRIG. GEN. JOSEPH M. HERNANDEZ

When Florida was ceded to America in 1821, a few prominent Spanish Floridian citizens transferred their allegiance to the United States. One of these was Joseph M. Hernandez (1792-1857) a native of St. Augustine. During 1822-23 he was the first congressional delegate from the new territory of Florida. He also ranked as a general in the Second Brigade of Florida Militia during the Seminole War and so was involved in Jesup's planning at Fort Mellon in 1837 for the campaign that culminated in the battles of Okeechobee that year and the Loxahatchee in early 1838.

Previously he had been active in protecting his sugar plantation, Mala Compra, at the head of Matanzas Lagoon. However, his was not the only plantation, as we are reminded today by such Florida state parks and historic sites as Bulow Plantation, Kingsley Plantation, and New Smyrna Sugar Mill, as well as Washington Oaks Gardens, the present historic site name for Hernandez's own plantation and his only geographic remembrance. In present Flagler and Volusia counties were centered a total of twenty-one sugar plantations, all of which were burned and destroyed by the Seminoles between

December 1834 and January 1836. Thus Hernandez was thrust into the unsavory execution of Jesup's command to entrap Osceola, Coacoochee, and others in this plantation area.

While Eustis was forging his way south to the west of the St. Johns, Hernandez was setting out from New Smyrna. His mounted men threaded their way through an unknown and never-before-visited tract of country between the St. Johns and Indian River. Jesup's message to Poinsett datelined "Headquarters Army of the South, Fort Mellon, November 29, 1837" states that "General Hernandez will turn Indian River with his mounted men, and pass the foot and supplies across. I shall not allow his operations, nor those of Colonel (Zachary) Taylor or General Smith, to be checked for a moment by the Seminoles councils; and the delay of this column will be more than counterbalanced by the increased efficiency of its means." In other words, Jesup was holding back his center-position St. Johns column pending the final report of the Cherokee Deputation while allowing the left and right columns to proceed; no doubt that is why the battle of Okeechobee was fought before Jesup arrived. It also took Hernandez longer than Taylor to get in position, so that the main contribution of Hernandez was logistical at the battle of the Loxahatchee, January 24, 1838. Hernandez's soldiers, who went down Indian River (as Motte described his own participation), arrived at Fort Jupiter the first week in January; having the advantage of carrying only baggage that could be packed on mules, they did not have to exert the effort that Eustis expended in moving his train of baggage wagons.

Hernandez's public career ended in 1845 when as a Whig he lost election to the United States Senate. Taking this rejection very seriously, he moved to Cuba and died there in 1857.[30]

As an epilogue to this chapter, it may be appropriate to point out that the ascription of names of forts to individuals has not been mere assumption. As a matter of record, the August 17, 1839, *Niles' National Register,* quoting the *Army and Navy Chronicle* and referring to the more than seventy-five forts established during the Second Seminole War, noted that these forts were named for those officers who had fallen victim to the foe or the climate as well as for living officers who had distinguished themselves. The writer then went on to cite a long list of such names, among them Mellon, Kingsbury, Lane, Peyton, McNeil, Maitland, and Gatlin. It was further noted that some of the seventy-five posts were then already abandoned, that some were merely stockades, and that others had scarcely any outward defenses. In the case of Fort Mellon the order that Fanning read at the burial of Charles Mellon provides clear documentation. On the other hand, it is apparent from the previous chapter that Fort Reid was named for a nonmilitary figure.

Chapter 11
Conclusion

E. FORBES.

One of the "Forty" 1841.

We can now draw some conclusions as to Fort Mellon's significance and importance. To Sanford residents, of course, Fort Mellon represents the American beginnings of their city; thus, they celebrate Founders Day each year on February 8, the anniversary of the battle of Camp Monroe.[1] This celebration was first held on the hundredth anniversary of the battle, in 1937, and it enjoyed a heightened emphasis in 1977, the centennial year of Sanford's incorporation.

The actual battle of Camp Monroe, it must be admitted, was not a major engagement, not even in terms of the Second Seminole War. Many other battles involved greater numbers and had a greater effect upon the course of the war. Yet had the garrison not repulsed the Seminole attack, there might well have been no Fort Mellon, and that circumstance would certainly have altered the army's subsequent logistical maneuvers. There can be no doubt that Fort Mellon was the staging area for the St. Johns wing of the 1837-38 campaign that resulted in the battles of Okeechobee and the Loxahatchee; by virtue of its central geographic location at the head of navigable water this site was the point of entry into the interior during the war (and after, until the railroad era).[2] The fort saw the first extensive logistical employment of steamboats in wartime, and it was included in some of the earliest army corps planning for the dredging of an inland river. Its position on Lake Monroe made it a base for exploration, too. During the fort's lifetime our knowledge of the upper St. Johns was extended by 100 miles; the river's course was charted, and a number of large lakes were discovered and named.[3]

Fort Mellon's central location also made it an important assembly point. It was the base of operations for the unsuccessful efforts of the Cherokee Deputation. Paddy Carr and his band of friendly Creeks were stationed at the fort, which was also visited by most of the leading Seminole chiefs, so that for a time in late 1837 it was home for members of three major Indian tribes: Seminole, Creek, and Cherokee. On the army side, Fort Mellon (including Fort Reid) was a military home for over one hundred commissioned officers, at least fifty-nine of whom were products of West Point; these figures offer compelling testimony as to the fort's importance as a military post. The twelve army surgeons who served at the fort provided the area with its first medical service.

Culturally, Fort Mellon was the scene of some early Florida examples of art and writing: the two pencil sketches by Vinton and the diary of Pickell. (We know that Motte's account was not written in the field and that he did not prepare to compose his book until 1845.) Allen Morris, in evaluating regional literature, thinks that Florida's beauties and adventures will figure as the elements that have inspired the state's most vigorous and moving writing.[3] Pickell did respond to these elements: he reported several kinds of plovers, quail, ducks, white and blue cranes, brant, and water turkeys, as well as trout, bream, catfish, sunfish, and alligators. Of flowers the coreopsis caught his attention; and he was impressed by "the Palmetto Grass and natural meadows hedged with evergreens" that "presented beautiful objects of scenery." He also noticed pearly shells and glowing sunsets, as well as thin strands of Spanish moss. The adventure of exploration and the novelty and uniqueness of the Indians were likewise subjects to which he was sensitive; and he expressed himself contemplatively on war and peace while enduring the asperity of army life. His was the earliest local literary endeavor, and by Allen Morris' criteria his efforts are not without merit. He seems to have done a better job at writing than at exploring, even though he probably felt the other way around.

Bert Collier, in writing his Florida Bicentennial newspaper series, made the point about William Bartram that "In one sense American Literature was born along the St. Johns River." In this connection we should remember that the St. Johns was also the parent of another literary effort, satirical in nature and dubious as to merit, but nevertheless of historical interest; it is presented in the following from a collection of army ballads.

THE MULE'S LAMENT

Know ye the land where the River St. John's
    Rolls on through the palm forest to the salt sea;
Where Sol gilds the mule yard when morning first dawns,
    And the sheds that give shade to my brothers and me?

Through its hummocks and forests, for many a day
    Have I toiled o'er the sands for my pitiful grain;
And sighed at my trough till my tail has grown gray,
    And sweat for my country again and again.

When the war whoop was heard in the pine shadowed wood;
    When the drivers all ran, and the fight was a race,
Like a Holy Cross knight in my harness I stood,
    Calmly smiling at fate, with my leg o'er the trace.

'Midst this donkey brevetment, oh! where my reward?
    Ungroomed and unshodden, faint, foundered, and sick:
The first transport that passes will bear me on board,
    Floating down the St. John's, to be sold at Black Creek.

My brothers in toil, yet uncrushed by the chains,
    Be warned by my fate — this your doom I foretell:
When the war trumpets cease, for your service and pains,
    You'll be sold at Black Creek by the auctioneer Bell.[4]

Some may ask whether the story of Fort Mellon should be retold, since the process of Indian removal does not show America at her best. Yet Sanford's early history was a movement of action and color depicted on the canvas of the local terrain. It should be viewed as a painting of historic merit — we do not criticize an artist because some of his characters are unesthetic. The mutual treachery of the Spanish and French has not dampened the accepted colorful historical picture of St. Augustine.

If we self-moralize, as is the wont of Americans in contrast to other nations, we might say that since Andrew Jackson was the official advocate of the Indian removal program, we perhaps should reevaluate his contribution to American democracy. From the viewpoint of broad and enlightened humanitarianism 140 years later, one might be obliged to say that Jackson's concern for humanity was too narrow. I have noted previously that after the acquisition of Florida from Spain the Seminoles were looking to the American government to offer some plan that would include them. Even General Jesup, expressing his own opinion about the Seminoles to the secretary of war ten days after the battle of Camp Monroe, said that "there would be no difficulty in making peace if they were allowed to remain in the country even as citizens, or individuals subjected to our laws; but many of them prefer death to removal."[5]

It would thus appear that the Seminoles were willing to coexist if they were given the same rights as the whites, which sentiment William Bartram had already observed forty-six years prior. That old sage and master of many subjects, at the end of the introduction to his 1791 *Travels,* was satisfied that the Indians "were desirous of becoming united with us in civil and religious society" and that the United States should "offer to them a judicious plan for their civilization and union with us."[6] This uncomplicated point, as applicable to the Seminoles, seems to have been missed by those who have over-rationalized and ascribed other, more complex causes for the failure to incorporate the Indians into American civilization. In view of the great numbers who emigrated to this country, one has to assume that the American melting pot could have operated for the Indians as it did for other ethnic influxes — for example, the proportion of blacks in America is much greater than the Indian element ever would have been. It is regrettable that neither Jackson nor the government was sufficiently magnanimous or prophetic to envision that this country could assimilate the Indians as peacefully as it did others at a later date. Naturally, this point is much clearer in retrospect.

Perhaps we can salve our consciences as did Capt. Nathaniel Wyche Hunter, an 1833 West Point graduate and the June 1841 commander of Fort Mellon, whose voice seems strikingly prophetic of our country's experience in this decade. Abhorring the tragedy of the Indians' "Trail of Tears" and expressing his own innate repugnancy to commit an outright act of murder or to premeditate the death of an Indian prisoner under his command, he admitted an obligation to his government but still desired some semblance of justice on his side. His soul-searching soliloquy might be considered the seldom-articulated conscience of Fort Mellon:

> I've tried every argument to still my conscience, but this restless imp will not be quiet. It bores me to death with impertinent questions relative to the propriety of conduct in which I am engaged and when I answer in the hackneyed phraseology of the day — that I have no right to discuss the propriety of my order; that it is the duty of a soldier to obey; that government is but enforcing a

:eaty; that our enemies are barbarous murderers of women and hildren; and last, that I am paid for acting not thinking—Sister to he audacious imp reply, "Fiat justitia ruat calm [caelum]."* Have ʒod and justice no claims upon you prior and paramount to a ;overnment that incites you to the commission of a crime? Will no :ompunctions deter you from wringing your hands in innocent ɔlood, even though it be the command of a superior officer? ᴣnforce a treaty, a compact begot in fraud and brought forth in the ɔlackest villainy and now in process of condemnation aided by the vilest machinations man or demon could invent? Is not every act of the Indians sanctioned by the practice of civilized nations? Are they not sanctioned by expediency and revenge? Mark me — if in this unhallowed surface one drop of Indian blood should soil your hands like Lady Macbeth you may cry to all eternity, "Out damned spot."[7]

*Let justice be done, though the heavens fall.

Appendix A
Col. A. C. W. Fanning's Official Report of the Engagement on February 8, 1837, at Camp Monroe on Lake Monroe, Florida

Camp Monroe, on Lake Monroe Florida
9th February 1837

General

On yesterday morning, a little before daylight, we were aroused by the war whoop all around us. The Enemy's right rested on the Lake above us, and his line extended round our front, his left resting on the lake below. Our men sprang to their breastworks. A sharp contest ensued. Second Lieut. Thomas of the 4th Arty was directed to go on board the Seamboat Santee, serve the six pounder, and direct his fire upon the right of the enemy. Our flank in that direction was soon cleared. The Enemy pertinaciously hung upon our front and right flank for nearly three hours and then retired, wearied of the contest. Our men, being recruits, at first wasted a great deal of ammunition, and it was with much difficulty the officers prevented them from throwing away their shots. They soon, however, became collected and in the end behaved extremely well. In fact the enemy was handsomely repulsed. The extensive fire of the enemy and the traces he has left behind, shew him to have been about from three to four hundred in force.

The melancholy part of my story remains to be related. The brave Captain Mellon of the 2nd Reg. of Artilly, a few minutes after the combat commenced, received a ball in his breast, and fell dead at his post. We, last night, gave to his remains, all we could give, our tears, and "a Soldiers grave." Capt Mellon entered the service at the commencement of the last war with England, and has ever since remained in it. He has left no property and I know he had left a widow and four children to deplore his loss. Their pension will be but twenty five dollars per month for five years. Now I think too well of my countrymen to believe it is their will that this should be the limit of the Nation's gratitude.

Passed Midshipman McLaughlin, serving with the Army, ready by my side to convey orders, received a ball in his breast. The Surgeon cannot yet pronounce his fate, but has strong hopes for his recovery. This gentleman had charge of the Supplies for the Detachment as well as of those for the Army expected here. He has performed his duties with great zeal and ability. On every occasion of apparent danger, I have found him on the spot, ready to perform any service of hazard. Let us hope he may yet live to grace the profession he has chosen.

On examining the ground, we found no dead enemies, yet we found several trails apparently made by the dragging off of dead bodies. We also found several belts and straps covered with blood, a small pouch of bullets and some scalping knives. It is most probable the enemy suffered more than ourselves. It is true we are without the trophies of victory, but this is no reason that the Officers whom I have had the honor to command and whose gallant bearing I have witnessed, should not receive honorable mention. Lieut. Col. Harney, commanding the four Companies of Dragoons, displayed during the contest, the greatest boldness and vigour, — and inspired his newly enlisted men with great confidence. I have at all times received from him the most energetic support. With the officers of his battalion I have every reason to be well satisfied. My eye was upon every one and I discovered nothing but firmness and confidence in all. In justice to them their names must be mentioned. Capt. Gordon, Capt. Bean, 1st Lieut. Jno Graham, 1st Lieut. Howe, 1st Lieut. Hamilton, 1st Lieut. Blake, 2nd Lieut. McNeil, 2nd Lieut. Thornton, 2nd Lieut. Kingsbury, and 2nd Lieut. May.

      On the fall of Capt. Mellon, Capt. Vinton of the 3rd Artilly assumed the command of the two Companies of Artillery. I have long known his high military attainments. On this occasion I witnessed his conduct and courage. 1st Lieut. Davidson took the command of Mellon's Company during the engagement. It could not have fallen into better hands. I have already spoken of the service renderd by 2nd Lt. Thomas of the 4th Arty. He has always volunteered his services on every dangerous scouting party. Lieut. Piercy of the Navy, Captain of the friendly Indians, with his indian force, fought among the regular troops; and he is always foremost in danger. He has at all times volunteered his services for any difficult or hazardous enterprise.

      Ast. Surgeon Laub dressed the wounded under the fire of the Enemy. In fact, I have never seen the sick soldier more promptly or faithfully attended to, then since this detachment left Volusia. Lieut. Dusenbery Quarter Master to the Expedition, had been sent previously to the attack, to Volusia and could not be present at the time. His duties have been very arduous and he has discharged them with vigor, zeal and ability. Paddy Carr, the Creek Chief, fought well. — He has generally headed the scouting parties, and has performed these laborious and dangerous duties with great promptitude and cheerfulness.

      I cannot end this letter without publicly expressing my thanks to Captains Brooks & Peck, of the Steam Boats Santee and Essayons. They have unhesitatingly pushed their boats through difficult channels and unknown waters, into the heart of the Enemy's country.

      I have mentioned all; it is because all deserve mention. Never was an officer, — charged with a delicate and hazardous enterprise, — served with more zeal and promptitude.

      You will herewith receive official lists of the killed & wounded. To the wounded, Passed Midshipman McLaughlin should be added. The "John Stoney" is just arrived. Lt. Dusenbery hands me a letter from Lieut. Chambers, ADCamp [aide-de-camp]. By this I learn that hostilities are to cease for the present, and that this detachment is directed to fall back upon Volusia.

                 I have the honor to be
                 General
                 Yr. Very Obt. Servt
                 A. C. W. Fanning
                 Bvt. Lt. Col. Comdg.
                 Detach.

Appendix B
Lt. John Pickell's "Brief Notes of the Campaign against the Seminole Indians in Florida, in 1837"

1837. Fort Heilman E. F.

Wednesday Nov. 8th. Arrived at Black Creek from Baltimore, which I left on the 31st. ult.

Sunday 12th. Commenced my duty as adjutant in the Field. Lt. Col. Bankhead commanding Fort Heilman. The weather since my arrival has been very pleasant. This evening 2 young Seminole warriors were brought to camp, having been captured by a party of Florida militia about 25 miles S. The effective force of the command at this post according to the Field Report made out to day is [blank space] The Dragoons 2nd. Regt under the command of Col. Twiggs commenced embarking to day: two & a half companies for Volusia. The remaining companies will embark for the same destination as fast as S. Boat conveyance up the St. Johns river can be afforded.

Monday 13th. This afternoon two more companies of Dragoons (2nd. Regt. embarked on Board the Steam Boat Cincinnati for Fort Mellon. The mail of to day brought me no letters. The weather continues pleasant.
A party of Florida mounted men returned from Rice creek & reported that they chased 8 Indians for some time & that they escaped by entering into a dense hammock.

Camp Heilman E. F. near Fort Heilman

Tuesday, Novr. 14th. Col. Twiggs left his encampment on the north side of Black creek with all the Dragoons excepting part of one company for Volusia.

Wednesday 15th. The preparations for moving continue.

Thursday 16th. The last company of the 2nd. Regt. Dragoons having left orders were issued to the troops under the command of Col. Bankhead to embark. The general was back at 3 o'clk P.M. and the command was marched to Garey's ferry for embarkation. Col. Bankhead & Adjt. with 34 of the mounted men under Lt. Allen and Companies "F" of 2nd. Arty & "D" 4th Arty. The officers Lt. Col. Bankhead commanding. Lt. Pickell adjt. 1st Lts. Ross & Whiteley. 2nd. Lts. Phelps, Pratt, Martin, Allen, Thomas & Dr. Maffit.
Comp "F." 2nd. Arty 57 Non. Coms & privates
Comp D 4th. Arty 50 Non. Coms & privates

Upon the S. Boat Santee were the remaining half of the mounted men of Capt. Ringgold's comp. now under the command of Lt. Allen and 2 Companies of the 3rd. Arty under Lt Col Gates. Upon the Steam Boat Forester, 3 Comps. of the 3rd. Arty.

The weather pleasant and by 6 o'clk
Friday morning Nov. 17th. we reached Volusia where we stopped for about one hour and visited the pickets. The post under the command of Bvt. Maj. J. L. Gardner 4th Arty. with 2 companies. The scenery along the banks of the St. Johns is thus far very monotonous. Before we entered Lake George [we noted] the growth upon the banks [;] we passed several Islands covered with Palmetto and Live oaks. The pickets at Volusia is located upon a bank of shells and the country bank to the hammock nearly one mile is composed of the same as also that on the opposite side far along the bank. Volusia is situated upon the S.E. side of Lake George. The pass between Lake George & Lake Monroe occasionally contracts and expands from 100 yds to ¾th of a mile in width. We entered into Lake Monroe at ¼ before 4 o'clk P.M. and arrived off Fort Mellon at ½ past 5 o'clk P.M. From the mouth of Lake Monroe to Ft. Mellon that was distinctly seen the direction is very little N. of E. distant about 4 miles. Being too late to land Col. Bankhead, Dr. Maffitt & myself went on shore, Lt. Col. Harney of the 2nd. Dragoons comdg., to ascertain the best position for the encampment. We passed the Steam Boat about 12 miles from Ft. Mellon. Col. Harney informed us that two days since he went out about 2 miles from the Fort and discovered signs of two or three Indians fresh. No Indians have been seen. The Fort occupies the ground which was a dense hammock when the Indians made their attack on the pickets in which Capt Mellon was killed about 8 months ago. The ground is high & composed of hillocks of the same kinds of shells as at Volusia. The situation is pleasant, facing upon Lake Monroe, a beautiful sheet of water.

Remarks — about 30 miles [upriver] of Volusia, passed the entrance of a stream into the St. John's called the Silver Spring which is remarkable for the clear and green-like color of the water. The line between the dark brown & green waters of the St. Johns & Silver Spring is beautifully striking to the view.

River Birds, wild Turkies, Ducks, several varieties of Cranes, Water Turkies, marsh hens and Alligators were seen in considerable numbers & afforded amusement to shoot them and particularly the Alligators. Lake Beresford is about 30 miles from Volusia. The Palmetto Grass and natural meadows hedged with evergreens presented beautiful objects of scenery. Our passage from Volusia to Ft. Mellon was very serpentine & several times in very short distances almost entirely turned every point of the compass. In the afternoon we had several little showers of rain. We remained on Board of the Boat until morning.

Saturday 18th. Landed the Troops, and encamped a little distance from the bank of Lake Monroe on a beautiful & gentle slope. Busy in arranging the encampment.

Sunday 19th. The S. Boat Charleston with Genl. Eustis arrived. Several showers of rain. An order for Comp 4th. Regt. Arty: and Companies, B, F & H of the 3rd. Arty. under the command of Lt. Col. Bankhead to proceed by sunrise tomorrow in the Steam Boats Santee & McLean to the highest accessible point of Lake Harney to establish a post on its West bank. The expedition is supplied with one Six poundr & 100 rounds of ammunition and the whole command with 100 musket ball & Buck shot cartridges each & 15 Signal rockets. The officers of the Command — Lt. Col. Bankhead, Lt. Pickell adjutant, Dr. Maffit, 1st. Lieuts. Davidson & Ross, 2nd. Lts. Tompkins, Mock, Phelps, Martin & Taylor.

Monday 20th. Struck our tents at sunrise and left Fort Mellon at ½ past 7 o'clk A.M. At the head of Lake Monroe we had considerable difficulty in getting over the bar at the mouth — having only 4 ft. water and the Santee drawing loaded a few inches more. At 4 o'clk we passed over the bar and the S. Boat McLean passed over immediately after. We reached by dusk about 5 miles from the bar — in all say 8 miles from Fort Mellon. It rained in showers until we anchored for the night. The country bordering upon the river thus far is savannahs with occasionally a grove of Palmettoes. Our course has been south easterly, the river meandering. The S. Boat McLean lays along side. Nothing has occurred that requires to be particularly noted. Before I left Ft. Mellon I wrote to my brother informing him of our intended expedition.

Tuesday 21st. At ½ past 11 o'clk A.M. arrived at our position about ½ a mile from the Western shore of the Lake and immediately after landed. The S. Boat anchored, had two boats manned with 20 men with arms in each boat and went on shore, in company with Col. Bankhead, Lieuts. Davidson, Ross, Tompkins and Dr. Maffitt to examine the ground for the establishment of a military post. Upon landing we found that the high land along the shore was a narrow belt of white sand covered with palmettoes and a few live oaks interspersed. Beyond was wet, marshy land, extending along parallel to the coast for about 7 miles and broken at one place by a very wet cypress swamp which we found impracticable to pass. No position could be found upon this bank suitable to the object in view. It was unapproachable on the South in consequence of the wet strip of land about 500 yards wide. Enough of palmates for the picketing but is favored for fuel; could not be approached by the Steam Boats nearer than 50 yds. with 4 ft. water and no water for drinking and cooking. In the afternoon Lts Davidson, Tompkins & myself again landed to make a more critical examination, and were confirmed in the opinion in which we all concurr'd that it was impracticable to make a location upon this part of the shore. We discovered two small running streams very saline falling into the lake about 3 miles apart. The remains of several Indians lodges, but which did not appear to have been occupied for some time past. Pieces of cloth and soldiers uniforms were found at the lodges and several hominy pounders used by the Indians. South of the ridge of sand we discovered a trail which runs nearly parallel to the shore and was no doubt at one time much used. The Indian track seemed to be but a day old going East. The ground had

117

every indication of having been much trodden by horses and cattle probably a week or ten days since. Wolf & deer tracks, at several places near the lake. An excellent canoe was discovered, a flat, and several planks along the shore. The men took possession of the canoe and brought it to the S. Boat.

Several beautiful flowers grew upon the ridge. The coryopsis particularly was abundant and exceedingly fragrant. The birds seen were several kinds of plovers, quail, ducks, white & blue cranes, Brant, black birds and some small birds. I obtained on the shore a specimen of thin strands of moss and several specimens of shells; the inside of which had a fine pearly appearance. The. bushes & grass along the shore showed that the water had been lately about 4 ft. higher than at present. The greatest length of the lake about 9 miles is nearly N. & S. The streams are literally filled with fish, trout, bream & sun fish. Large Catfish were caught to day by some of the men from the S. Boats. The view to the East is an interminable savannah, covered with a luxurious growth of grass. I returned to the S. Boat after sun set much fatigued with the examination we had made. During the day we had several showers of rain some heavy. The sun set was the most perfectly glowing I have ever seen.

Wednesday 22nd. At day light this morning I went with the captains of the S. B. Santee and McLean to sound the bar at the head of Lake Harney with the view of going up the river with the McLean as far as practicable. The country on the western shore not being at all suitable for a military depot, Col. Bankhead was induced from the favorable appearance of the character of the country higher up the river to examine the ground bordering upon it and to ascertain whether a more favorable position could be obtained for the proposed depot. Upon a careful sounding we found 3 ft. 8 inches over the bar, a sufficient depth for the McLean if lightened by removing the surplus wood, etc. to the Santee. We weighed anchor at 9 o'clk A.M. and passed over the bar without difficulty, and were again under weigh up the river at ¼ after 10 o'clk P.M. After proceeding 7 or 8 miles we grounded on 3 ft. 6 inches. Anticipating much delay in getting off which could only be affected by taking out the wood and loading I proposed to Col. Bankhead to dispatch the yawl Boat with a few hands, etc. under my direction to proceed up the river to examine it. At about 4 o'clk I started in the Boat with Capt. Curry of the McLean his mate and two hands. At a short distance from the S. Boat we entered a Lake 1¼ miles long, and within the next 3 miles two other lakes of nearly the same size. These lakes were united by the straits of the river 3 or 400 yards long. After leaving the last lake we ascended the river about one mile further; the river from the lake last noted is contracted to a width of 7 or 9 yards with the shore bold. The water [is] from 3 to 7 ft. in depth and the banks covered with a high serge [sedge]. At the termination of this reach, it opened into a beautiful lake nearly circular and of about 1 mile diameter. This lake is evidently the head water of the St. John river and which terminates in the midst of the everglades, so celebrated as the terra incog. and which perhaps never before had been so far penetrated "by white man" and perhaps never by the "red man." The head of the river is in a southeasterly direction from the head of Lake Harney and distant from 15 to 16 miles. The appearance of the

118

everglades is interesting and spreading out E & West from the head of the river 15 or 20 miles, dotted with three or four small groups of palmettoes. Towards the South the river is interminable.

The Everglades are extensive savannahs covered with high grass and checkered over with branches and ponds. Upon the summit the ground is very level and the grass grows to the height of 10 to 12 feet. That bordering the head Lake is a species of red serge [sedge] and differs from the growth farther down the river. Water fowl were very plenty and never before were started from their green retreats by the noise of the boatman's paddle. The most numerous of the fowl kind was the Curlew, which were of the white and brown species. Ducks, water hens were also numerous. After having critically coursed and examined the bank of the Lake we commenced our return at dark and reached the S. Boat at 9 o'clk P.M. In consequence of the lateness the Bell of the S. Boat was rung to advise us of its position, which we heard when about 3 miles from it. On our return, I had of course much to relate of the exploration. I was careful in sketching the part of the river above the S. Boat to the head of the River and took minute notes, adding my notes and sketches to those of Lieut. Davidson who accompanied the party. We were enabled after my return to make a correct map of the river and everglades from Lake Harney to the head of the river, and which we presented to Col. Bankhead. We remained in the river until next morning.

Thursday 23rd. At sunrise we were on our return to the Lake and which we reached the anchorage over the bar at about 9 o'clk A.M. and by 12 N. were under weigh to the outlet of the Lake towing the Santee. At 1 P.M. the McLean was dispatched with a communication from Col. Bankhead to Genl. Eustis at Fort Mellon giving an account of our expedition and the result of the examination of the ground at the head of the Lake and to the head of the river, and recommending that another position be fixed upon as more favorable for a Depot. We dropped down from the mouth of the Lake ¾th of a mile and fastened the Boat to the shore at ½ an hour before sun set. Here the men had an opportunity of cooking on the shore and remained on the shore until nearly 8 P.M. At 9 P.M. two signal rockets were fired off. Towards the S.E. smoke was discovered at several places. The fires were beyond the woods bordering the lake, apparently 10 miles from us. Last night and this morning uncomfortably cold. In consideration of having discovered the head of the St. John's river, Col. Bankhead did me the honor of naming the Lake at its source Lake Pickell and accordingly write it upon the map. I forgot to say that the St. John's river is supplied by the rain that falls upon the level ground at the summit in the everglades which contains numerous natural reservoirs. From the appearance of the grass the water has recently been 18 inches deep upon the general surface of the ground.

Friday 24th. This morning despatches were recd. from Genl. Eustis and Col. Bankhead directed the S. Boats to run up to the head of the Lake for the purpose of sending 2 Barges up the river with the Negro guide Ben to the upper crossing said to be about 25 miles from the Lake. Lt. Ross and myself had each

119

charge of a Barge accompanied by Lieut Tompkins and 30 men. We left the Bar at ¼ after 4 o'clk P.M. and by 8 o'clk we were in Lake P. and were obliged to return about one mile to get into another channel. We ran our boats to shore and at 9 o'clk put up two Signal rockets as agreed upon when we arrived at our destination, but which we understood to be given when we stopped for the night. It was answered by the S. Boat on the Lake by one rocket. The night was very cold and of course our sleep was not very refreshing.

Saturday 25th. At day light we were again under way and at ½ past 11 o'clk A.M. reached the main crossing about 25 or 27 miles above the Lake. At a point 7 miles below we landed and visited a small Indian habitation on a shell hillock which we found under cultivation. Pumpkins and Cabbages were growing upon it. No evidence of Indians having been at it for the last 10 or 12 days. This hillock was on the W. side and 4 or 500 yds from the landing. At the upper crossing we also landed, and waded through a pond 200 yds wide & 3 & four feet deep we reached a palmetto grove and several Indian lodges. Here we found quite an extensive cultivation of Sweet Potatoes, peppers, pumpkins, etc. The Indians had just left it, as the fire was burning and the potato vines seemed to have been just dug up. I brought from it a branch of an orange tree. At noon we left on our return to the Lake and which we reached at ½ after 4 P.M. having been about on the expedition 24 hours. Water fowl abounded and seemed to have increased as we ascended. The character of the country is savannah with occasional groves of palmettoes. Returning to the lake we met the S. Boat about 4 miles up. In consequence of our signal rockets having indicated to Col. B. that we had arrived at our destination at 9 o'clk last night, and not returning in the morning Col. B. and those below were apprehensive that we had met with some serious difficulty, and therefore they moved up the river.

Sunday 26th. At day light we left the head of the Lake for the outlet where we arrived by 7 o'clk A.M. Col. Bankhead directed me to proceed in the S. Boat McLean to Ft. Mellon with dispatches for Genl. Eustis. We started at 8 A.M. and at ½ past 11 A.M. arrived at Ft. Mellon. On my arrival I ascertained that a family of Indians had come in the day before and gave favorable accounts of the intentions of the Indians to come in after a talk was held between the several chiefs and warriors. It is said that Micanopy had directed that there should be a meeting at Powells creek about 60 miles from Fort Mellon. I am inclined to the opinion that the last rifle has been fired and this opinion is strengthened by the fact that on coming down the river from the upper crossing there was afforded hundreds of opportunities from the natives of the country to have shot upon us undiscovered & of which they did not avail themselves. This I ascribe to their intention not to fire another rifle. So much for a digression.

Having recd. my orders from Genl. Eustis I started on my return to Col. Bankhead's command at the outlet of Lake Harney. Genl. Eustis directed that we should return as soon as possible to Ft. Mellon and more than probable a floating depot will be made at the head of Lake H. and Col. B's command will be directed to move up the St. Johns to its highest point. Left the wharf at Ft. M. at ½ past 4 P.M. and arrived at the outlet of Lake H. at ½ after 7 P.M. The officers were all anxiously awaiting my return to hear what would be the destination of our command. All are in favor of the expedition up the St. John's river, and which could then be explored to its head.

Monday 27th. At 10 min. of 10 o'clk A.M. we got under way for Ft. Mellon.

I omitted to state in my yesterday's notes that the Cherokee delegation had arrived at Fort Mellon. Genl. Jessup with Col. Twiggs command of 2nd Regt. of Dragoons, and Major Gardner with 2 Companies of the 4th. Artillery from Volusia arrived also at about noon yesterday. On my way down the weather was very pleasant & the atmosphere clear and the water and land checkered over with groves of palmetto presented a fine view. On my return in the evening the sunset was particularly glowing, and rich. We found much difficulty in getting the Santee over the bar and shallows of the river and did not reach the mouth of the river at the head of Lake Monroe until nearly 2 o'clk P.M. Finding it impossible to get the S. B. over the bar Col. Bankhead and myself went on board the McLean that had already crossed and proceeded in her to Fort Mellon and where we arrived at 3 o'clk P.M. After the two companies on board had landed she returned to the Santee with several lighters to take off what was necessary to reduce her draught of water to cross the bar.

Tuesday 28th. The Santee did not suceed in coming over the bar until about noon today. The arrangements with the delegation of the Cherokee chiefs having been made for their departure, they left the camp at 2 o'clk P.M. to meet the Seminole Chiefs in Council at Powell creek said to be 50 miles distant in a S. Westerly direction. After going through the ceremony of shaking hands they mounted their horses and rode slowly through the camp. The delegation 5 in number headed by the celebrated Seminole Chief Co-a-hadjo, attired in the rich costume of his nation, presented an imposing spectacle and left us with our best wishes for their success in their errand of peace. God grant they may succeed and prevail upon the hostile chiefs to come in, and yield without further bloodshed to the necessity which they cannot by any means obviate. The opinion of the officers is that the delegation will be successful. It is expected to return by Saturday next. That day so important to our future operations, is awaited with the most patient anxiety.

Wednesday 29th. At 10 o'clk A.M. Col. Bankhead's command is ordered on an excursion of 3 or 4 miles for the sake of recreation. As the command was forming on the grand parade we had a shower of rain and several showers while on the march. We proceeded about 3 miles and returned to camp by 1 o'clk P.M. An order was issued for a general court martial to convene at this post tomorrow. Genl. Eustis President & Lt. Davidson Judge Advocate. Awakened by the Santee which leaves tomorrow. The wolves for the last two nights have made much noise around our encampment. Their barking to those who have not heard them before in an Indian country would take it to

121

be the terrible yelling of the Savages. Such it seemed to me at first, but being now accustomed to their noise it is easily distinguished from the yell of the Indians.

Thursday 30th. At 11 o'clk A.M. a detachment of recruits 120 or 130 arrived from the New York rendezvous under Lieuts Allen & Lincoln. Several days ago an Indian runner was sent out at the request of Oseola who is a captive in St. Augustine, to bring in his family. Their arrival has been expected for the last three days, but did not arrive until 4 o'clk this afternoon. They came with a white flag, hoisted upon a staff or pole 8 feet high and presented altogether a pitiable sight. The bearer of the flag was a fine looking young warrior and at the head of the train, which was composed of about 50 souls including the two wives of Oseola and his two children & sister, 3 warriors and the remainder negro men women & children. The negro part of the train was a wretched picture of squalid misery. I have just received (8 o'clk P.M.) an order to have 12 privates & 2 non-commissioned officers detailed to guard them to St. Augustine and they will leave in the S. Boat at reveille tomorrow morning.

They say, to avoid meeting with the Indians who are hostile, they were obliged to leave the trail. They have been on their way a number of days and were much fatigued when they arrived; they brought two miserable looking Indian ponies with them. From the voraciousness of their appetites when they were supplied with food, they seemed to have been nearly starved. They inform us, that Sam Jones, or A-bi-a-ca, is about 30 miles from us, with several hundred warriors and is determined not to surrender, but give us battle in the open pine woods in which he has his present position. They did not see the Cherokee delegation, but came upon its trail after it passed them. They appeared much surprised at the number of troops we have here. They expected to see but a few soldiers. They also state that they saw us when we were up the river in the S. Boat, but too much fatigued to get to us, in time, and which they were anxious to do.

Friday, December 1st. By the order last evening the Indians and negroes, that surrendered themselves yesterday were to have left for St. Augustine immediately after reveille, did not leave until 9 o'clk A.M. in the Steam Boat for Picolata where they would be furnished with waggons to carry them to St. Augustine. The Indians were very reluctant to leave; they did not relish the idea of going on board of the "fire Boat" and even Oseola's family manifested rather an indisposition to go to St. Augustine. We hear nothing more from the Indians today. The two negroes that were kept as guides were further interrogated and they repeated in substance what they had said yesterday. To the question What number of Indian warriors Sam Jones or A:bi:a:ca had with him Negro Sampson replied that A:bi:a:ca had them all collected that is the several tribes, and they amounted to 1900. This is doubtful, as it exceeds the number it is stated by others.

This is the first day of winter and I cannot but reflect upon the contrast of the weather in this sunny climate, and that of the north. The air is soft and delightful; the woods are green, and the ground covered with all varieties of beautiful and fragrant flowers. At the north, I presume winter has set in with all the frosts and snows that belong to its latitudes. The woods have long since been stript of its foliage and the earth covered with its deep mantle of snow. Here no fires are required, for the air is as mild and pleasant as in the balmy month of May. At the north, the domestic hearth blazes with a cheerful fire and the fire-side is made still more pleasant by social intercourse by which hour after hour is beguiled with the time of retirement. Here the bed is the ground, with one solitary blanket to intercept the heavy dew which falls like a drizzling shower during the night. Tomorrow we will look for the return of the Cherokee Delegation. If they will not have succeeded, on Monday next we strike our tents and march to meet the enemy.

Saturday Decr. 2nd. The Steam Boat Cincinnati arrived this afternoon from Black creek and brought the unfortunate intelligence of the escape of 20 Indians from their confinement in the Fort in St. Augustine, among which were Wild Cat, or Co-a-coo-chee one of the most inveterate and hostile of the chiefs and Philip's son. They made their escape on Wednesday night, through the embrasures of the casemates in which they were confined and lowered themselves from the outside 14 or 16 ft. to the ground. This will we apprehend have an unfavorable effect upon the termination of the war, and particularly if they have been able to reach A-bi-a-ca's camp, before the Cherokee delegation will have concluded its "talk" with the hostile chiefs assembled in council at Powell's creek. If the council was held as early as was expected when the delegates left our camp on Tuesday last and which is supposed to have been concluded yesterday, they have not had time to reach it, as they must necessarily have travelled slowly in consequence of their long confinement and cautiously to escape apprehension, as no doubt they were immediately pursued upon learning that they had made their escape on Thursday morning.

Sunday Dec 3rd. The Steam Boat McLean arrived at 10 o'clk A.M. from Black creek. About 5 o'clk P.M. information reached Camp that the Cherokee Delegation with about 20 warriors & chiefs were within 5 miles on their way to our encampment, Micanopy at their head. I received orders to have the assembly sounded and the soldiers were immediately paraded under arms in the company parades. Soon after sunset the delegation appeared accompanied by Micanopy, Little Cloud and about 20 warriors with a white flag. They were escorted to the commanding General's tent after the chiefs had dismounted and shook hands. After a few questions were answered they retired to the tent that was pitched for them, and were informed that tomorrow morning a "talk" would be held with them. The delegation met them 50 miles distant and were received kindly. Another party of the hostiles is expected in tomorrow morning. A:bi:a:ca, or Sam Jones not being well enough to ride the distance, he sent his nephew as his representative and who came with the party, with the information that if Genl. Jessup would treat him well and send one of the Cherokees to him with that pledge he would come in with all his warriors amounting to about 400. Co-a-hadjo also accompanied the return of the delegation. The command under Col. Bankhead up the river was seen by the Indians and had an intention to make an attack upon us while we were either in Boats up the river or while we had landed from the S. Boat at the head of Lake Harney. If they had attacked us while exploring above the head of the Lake, the advantages they possessed would have enabled them to do us very serious injury. It was reported in camp today that the reports of Cannon were heard in a S.W. direction. The tent the Indians occupy is 25 or 30 yds. from mine. At 10 o'clk P.M. I looked at them around their fires. It was a novel sight. They appeared to be cheerful or occasionally they laughed outright at joking with each other.

Monday 4th. At 9 o'clk 10 more warriors came in, and at 1 o'clk P.M. 3 more and at 4 o'clk P.M. 3 more warriors arrived in Camp, making altogether 16 warriors that came in today. The last 3, say they are from E.Con-laik-hatchee creek which empties into the St. Johns river about 2 miles above Lake Harney. This day has been one of considerable anxiety, as the officers were generally of opinion that the army ought to have moved toward A-bi-a-ca. My opinion is that early this morning one of the Cherokee delegation ought to have been sent out to A-bi-a-ca, informing him that if he would surrender unconditionally he, and his warriors would be well treated, and that if they were so disposed they could meet us on the march or on his own ground, that we did not wish to destroy them, but only to abide by the provisions of the treaty and surrender themselves and emigrate. Parleying with the Indians gives them only hopes that cannot be fulfilled, and that if they fired one solitary rifle or made resistance they would be dealt with as enemies in arms against us. Promptness in this respect in my opinion would have had the effect we all most earnestly desire — an unconditional surrender and consequently a termination of hostilities. The Commanding General has no doubt acted at this important crisis upon the most mature deliberation, and after weighing in his mind the consequences that might result from the several modes that presented themselves to his mind from all the lights with which he has been furnished. I must confess, that my belief in the sincerity of the Indian Chiefs who have come in with the exception of Micanopy and Co-a-hadjo is a little impaired by their apparent indifference & manner here. I hope I am mistaken. It is reported that a Cherokee will leave to night for A-bi-a-ca's camp to carry the "talk" to him. If A-bi-a-ca is sincere, he will come in or meet us on our march and deliver up his army. He is considered the most important chief after Oseola and his inveteracy to the whites is said even to exceed that of the captive chief in St. Augustine.

It was reported that a "talk" would be held this evening, but nothing has been done. We are laying upon our oars and quietly looking ahead to the shore which unless some movement is made, we can never reach — the termination of the difficulties with the Seminoles.

Tuesday 5th. This morning the S. Boat Santee arrived and at about 4 o'clk P.M. the S. B. Camden. At noon the "talk" was held with the chiefs and warriors, on the area in front of Genl. Jessup's tent. Micanopy, Cloud, Tus-ke-gee &

others took their seats on benches. Micanopy was seated in the middle of his council chiefs. Cloud & Co-a-hadjo on his left and Tus-ke-gee & one other on his right. The replies to the interrogation of the Commanding Genl. were made by Micanopy, who occasionally consulted his chiefs before a question was answered. The "talk" did not seem to me to be entirely sincere on the part of the chiefs, although the questions were generally answered without much hesitation. The questions were propounded by Genl. Jessup and in much detail. Micanopy pledged himself that if Indian runners were allowed to go out to A-bi-a-ca, Jumper and the other chiefs that they would come in with their warriors and surrender their arms. As a guarantee for the fulfillment of this promise the Commanding General required that the women and children of the Indians that were nearest the camp should at once be brought in and also, the women & children of the captives in St. Augustine. The several chiefs selected the runners and they left our camp at 5 o'clk P.M. on horseback with the necessary supply of provisions for the time allowed to them to return. The runner to A-bi-a-ca is directed to get back in 7 days. The runner to Jumper in 10 days, and another to return in 10 days. I rode out a few miles this afternoon, in company with several officers and met a young warrior on his way to camp. He said that there was another near him, but who was afraid to come in. The one we met was a nephew of Co-a-hadjo. Upon telling him that Micanopy & other chiefs were in camp and that they would be treated well he went back for his companion and both then proceeded to Camp. Tomoka John and one of our interpreters (negro) were also met and they informed us that 4 Indians, 2 of the Tallahassee tribe were about 5 miles out, but they could not be prevailed upon to come with them to camp, and would allow them only to approach near enough to talk with them. An order is just issued for a court martial. Col. Bankhead President for the trial of Lieut Howe of the 2nd Regt. Dragoons. Weather continues pleasant.

Wednesday 6th. Genl. Jessup & staff left at 10 o'clk for Black creek to organize the Troops there, from Georgia, Alabama & Tennessee for service. Several Indians came into camp this morning.

Thursday, 7th. Steam Boat James Adams left for Black creek and Charleston. This day has had few incidents to make it distinguished. The day was cloudy and an occasional drizzling of rain. A Uchee Indian came in this morning and this evening as Dr. Maffitt and myself were riding along the trail a few miles from Camp we met a family of Co-a-hadjo's people — man woman & three children coming to camp. They were the most miserable and starved looking creatures that have yet presented themselves. They arrived in camp and after getting something to eat for them, they were allowed to go out to their wigwam under the promise of returning in the morning.

Friday, 8th. The Indian family returned to camp. The Steamer Camden left at 10 o'clk A.M. with Lieut. Lincoln and his company (64) of recruits. The S. Boat Cincinnati arrived at 3 o'clk P.M. from Black creek; brought nothing — that is, no letters.

Saturday 9th. The S. Boat Cincinnati left at noon for Black creek. Five Indians came in this morning. Two of these were taken down to Lake George with Genl. Jessup a few days ago where they said a small party of Indians resided & that they could prevail upon them to come to camp. They returned with 3 of them. They state that upwards of 40 Indians will be in tomorrow, they camp at a swamp about 15 miles distant tonight. The thermometer at 12 M. stood at 94° above zero – sun exposure. At 2 o'clk P.M. in the shade at 82° above zero – and after having laid a short time on the ground, it rose to 104°.

Sunday 10th. The Steam Boats McLean & Santee arrived today, brought no letters, both having left Black [creek] on the evening before the arrival of the mail. The wolves made a tremendous howling last night.

A party of Indians including 7 warriors – the rest women & children arrived in camp at 10 o'clk P.M. At 4 o'clk P.M. Col. Bankhead, Major Lomax & myself rode out about 3 miles and came to an Indian camp where we found 2 warriors and 8 or 10 women & children; they will be in our camp tomorrow. Provisions have been sent out to them. Upwards of 40 sticks were sent in yesterday, which indicates the number of Indians on their way & within one day's march of camp.

Monday 11. No arrivals of Indians today. Bushy-head one of the Cherokee delegation not coming in yesterday is a favorable circumstance, as it was understood if Abiaca did not consent to come to the camp with his warriors, he was to have returned yesterday. The fine looking young warrior, a nephew of King Philip, who asked permission on the day of the council to go out for the cattle that belong to him, and for what Genl. Jessup agreed to pay a just price, if they were retained in camp, has not yet returned as he had stated he would. He will probably return with Abiaca.

The Steam Boats Forester & Santee arrived this afternoon from Black creek. Genl. Jessup and staff returned in the Santee. Recd. a letter from Genl. Weightman.

This day has been cool and a fire in the morning & evening quite comfortable. Gen. Hernandez' command on the opposite side of the Lake and announced its arrival there by firing three times. Yesterday the Band of music belonging to the 2nd Regt Dragoons arrived from Garey's ferry & for the last two nights we have been favored with their fine music. Rode out with several officers to the Indian encampments two or three miles distant, no new arrivals of Indians at any of them.

Tuesday 12th. Bushy Head one of the Cherokee delegation and one of Cloud's Indians came at dusk this evening. Bushy-head was not as successful as we had wished. A-bi-a-ca does not appear to be disposed to surrender. Jumper says he will come in but is lame and cannot walk fast. Genl. Jessup will send a horse to him. After Bushy-head's return to camp a "talk" was held in front of Genl. Jessup's tent, at which Micanopy, Cloud and several of the sub-chiefs attended. The General gave the Chiefs to understand that no more time can be lost and that Co-a-coo-chee, Tus-ke-nug-gee, Miceo and one other must be surrendered at once, and that he would not listen to terms of peace unless they were brought in. The return of Bushy head produced a considerable excitement in camp. We had been expecting him since morning. His return would bring up intelligence of an important character and which would determine the character of our operations. If the Indians would come in with him, no more blood would be shed. If they refused and persisted in their hostilities they would be met as enemies in war and be dealt with accordingly.

Bushy-head and Mr. Fields two of the Delegation are determined if the hostiles can be prevailed upon to yield, to leave no efforts untried. They will leave to night and expect to be with Abiaca by 11 o'clk tomorrow morning. Bushy head said the last words he spoke to A-bi-a-ca when he found he was not willing to yield to his persuasions was ["]Well, Abiaca the consequences will be upon your head. The blood that will be shed you will be answerable for, if you will not regard my advice, farewell."

Wednesday 13th. Last night we had several hard showers of rain, and it continued raining until 10 o'clk A.M. after which it cleared off, and the weather continued very pleasant. At 5 o'clk P.M. it was reported that 2 of the Indians were missing. A party was sent after them but they did not succeed in finding them. One of them was a ferocious looking half negro and the other a nephew of A-bi-a-ca. Three warriors and 7 or 8 women & children came in this afternoon.

The Steam Boat Forrester left early this morning for Black creek.

An order was issued yesteray placing General Hernandez' Command under Genl. Eustis, and dividing the whole military force in Florida into two divisions, under Generals Armistead & Eustis.

Thursday 14th. At 7 or 8 o'clk this morning Bushy-head and Mr. Fields returned and brought unfavorable intelligence. The Indian that came in with Bushy-head on Tuesday evening accompanied them back towards A-bi-a-ca's camp and when within a mile or two of it told them that they need go no farther, that he was authorized by A-bi-a-ca to tell a lie to the white people and that Abiaca had left his camp and did not intend to come in, but was ready to give them battle whenever they came to his country. As soon as the Indian had made this statement and they found he had practiced deception, they left him without proceeding further and returned to our camp with this unexpected intelligence. Immediately after the Indians, women children & negroes amounting to 72 souls were collected. The guard was doubled and arrangements made for sending them to St. Augustine. This party including Micanopy and Co-a-hadjo numbered about 30 warriors or fighting men. 24 rifles were taken from them and secured. They embarked on board Steam Boat Santee at 2 o'clk P.M. with a guard of 18 men, 2 non-commissioned officers under the command of Lieut. Jones of the 3rd Arty. An order issued for 4 companies of the 3rd Arty and 2 companies of the 2nd. Regt. Dragoons under the command of Major Lomax, to take up the line of march at sun rise and open a waggon road along the trail round the head of Lake Jessup to the head of Lake Harney. The rest of the army will follow in all probability on

Saturday morning. A report reached camp this morning that several Indians were seen a short distance outside the line of Sentinels. Yesterday we felt as if it was a time of peace — today as it truly is a time of war. By the Steam Boat Santee left [words crossed out]. Since the departure of the Indians, the camp is comparatively quiet. And were we not preparing for the march which occupies our time, pretty constantly to day we might say that the camp is also less interesting. There was even until this day some novelty in the character, manners and customs of the Indian which amused and interested. The groups around their fires, women cooking sofka. The men making moccasins and the boys shooting through the reed at small oranges and numerous other novelties of the "redman" that almost constantly attracted attention. Even the dress of the chiefs and warriors with their wampum, leggins and frock fancifully decorated and ornamented and their party-colored turbans crowned with feathers and silver bands with their dignified step and gesture and their occasionally good humor'd frivolities were all so many sources of interest to us, that now, it has left a blank, which would be still more observed, were it not for the excitement attendant upon the preparation for the march. It is said that "Cloud" was much affected when he got on board the Steam Boat, that he actually shed tears, but as he had a villainous look, my opinion is that the tears were more on account of the impossibility of making his escape than anything else. We are all of opinion in as far as I have been able to know the opinion of the officers that Micanopy was in all he promised sincere. The noble looking chief Co-a-hadjo was probably equally sincere in all his professions of peace and friendship.

There are a number of incidents connected with an encampment that renders it interesting, especially upon such ground as we now occupy. Our encampment is on a gentle slope and about 300 or 400 yds from the lake. In front is the Dragoon encampment and on the right and left open pine woods interspersed with a few live oaks and palmettos on the flanks. At night groups of officers collect around fine blazing fires and talk over perhaps the occurrences of the day or discuss "matters and things in general" socially. The nature of the conversations is given according to circumstances, as the conversation is to pass time the most pleasantly, the subject changes perhaps one hundred times in the course of an evening. Thus time is agreeably and pleasantly passed until it is time to retire to our tents for rest.

How often do I think of my friends and of "home," where all the comforts and conveniences of life are richly enjoyed. The life of a soldier in the abstract is one of toil, care, anxiety and excitement; his fare coarse and simple, but withall he is content and is sustained only by the hope that his discomforts inconveniences, privations and hardships will have an end, and that he will at the termination of his service return to his friends, with the satisfaction that he has faithfully performed his duties in the cause in which his country has called him.

Friday, 15th. The command under Major Lomax left at 7 o'clk this morning. The weather pleasant the sky unclouded and a fine bracing breeze from the north, a very favorable day to begin the march.

This is certainly the most uninteresting day we have since we encamped here. The Indians gone, no Steam Boat arrived. The weather as usual, no incidents, no circumstances that are worthy of being recorded. It is only remarkable, because nothing has occur'd of sufficient interest to make a remark of in the Journal. We are anxiously expecting a Steam Boat from Black creek, which will bring us the Monday's mail.

Saturday, Dec. 16th. The Steam Boat Camden left at 9 o'clk A.M. with the Cherokee Delegation for Black creek. The negotiations of the Delegation as mediating between the hostile Indians and the government has been entirely unsuccessful. The Indians played a deep *ruse de guerre* by the deception they practiced upon the delegation and upon the army. The delay it has caused, they have availed themselves of, no doubt either to move farther south and to a country still more inaccessible to the Army, or otherwise strengthened themselves, while we were quietly awaiting the fulfillment of their promises & pledges at the day that was designated at the "talk."

Every disposition has been manifested on the part of the Commanding General to promote the object of the Delegation and to induce the Indians to surrender, without further resistance and which would result unavoidably to the serious injury of Indians as a people & as a nation. This we are all exceedingly desirous to avoid and had hoped the Cherokee Delegation who have no doubt very honestly and sincerely used every exertion to prevail upon A-bi-a-ca (Sam Jones) the most important & influential Chief of the hostiles to yield to their wishes and prevent the farther affusion of blood, and perhaps their extermination as a people. The consequences of their continued resistance has been represented to them. They are aware of what will follow. The Commanding General distinctly informed the runners when they went out, that if one drop of blood was shed by any one of them, the captives would be executed, & that it would most assuredly be carried into effect.

Of the origin of the war, it does not enter into the character of these daily notes, to inquire, but in justice to the Commanding General it is due to state that every indulgence every persuasion every means consistent with the policy of the government has been regarded and used to terminate, without the alternative of arms, this protracted war by the mediation of the Cherokee Delegation to which the War Department has given much importance by its sanction and acceptance. We are now on the eve of another campaign. Maj. Dearborn with 2 companies of the 2nd Infantry embarked on board of 2 Barges and 1 Lighter for the head of Lake Harney with provisions. He will proceed to the position occupied by Col. Bankhead's command on the 23rd ult. where the Army will repair to, should it become necessary to supply it with provisions from that quarter. An order is issued for Col. Bankhead's command consisting of detachments of the 3rd & 4th Artillery and Capt. Washington's Company to take up the line of march at sunrise tomorrow morning and join the advance part of the Brigade — the command to take 4 days provisions. The field Report of today that will march is 682 officers & soldiers — 24 soldiers will be left on account of sickness.

129

Appendix C
Lt. William B. Davidson's Marginal Notes to Army Map L247-2 "Téatre of Military Operations in Florida during 1835, 36, & 37"

Davidson's commentary apparently was not done in one sitting, as his notes are neither always chronological nor connected. Nevertheless, they comprise three main subjects: the American discovery of lakes Jessup and Harney, including the charting of the St. Johns from Fort Mellon; the feasibility of establishing a post (Fort Lane) on Lake Harney; and a description of General Eustis' march from Fort Mellon on December 17, 1837, to Fort Lane, to Fort Christmas, reached Christmas Day, to Fort McNeil, and finally to Fort Taylor, which was reached too late to assist actively in the battle of Okeechobee. Davidson also included a little mileage table showing the relative distances between the above forts. The January 8 and 9 (1838) notes presaged the imminent battle of the Loxahatchee on January 24, which with Okeechobee was the culmination of the fall-winter, 1837-38, logistical buildup at Fort Mellon.

The spelling "Téatre" for theater was probably a vestige of French military influence, as exemplified by Gen. Winfield Scott's aping of European methods of warfare and his attention to the French-inspired drill manuals at that time used by the United States Army.

The following begins at the right-hand top margin of the map.

Lake Jesup, about 8 miles long and formed like a crescent was discovered by Lieut Peyton 2nd Art, who ascended the St John to that Lake with a detachment of Art on the 22nd May 1837.

Nothing was known of the St Johns beyond that, until the 10th Novb following, when it was proposed by Lieut Col Harney & Lt Wm B. Davidson to attempt a further exploration of the St Johns with a view to ascertain whether it afforded any additional facilities for the transportation of supplies and the establishment of Depots. Accordingly on the 10th Nov. they started in the steamer Santee with Compy F 2nd Art [?] from Fort Mellon, and after dragging a little over the bar at the head of Lake Monroe, proceeded up the river without the least obstruction for 30 miles, where they discovered another large and beautiful lake 8 miles long & 5 or 6 wide, to which was given the name of Harney.

The boat was steamed round near the Eastern shore of the Lake and a landing made with 20 men in a barge, opposite to an indian Village situated in a beautiful Grove of Live Oaks and Palmettoes, about 3 miles from the entrance to the Lake.

The village appeared to be abandoned but a day or two before.

The Santee could not be forced over the bar at the head of the Lake and we returned by the Western shore, [and] arrived at F Mellon a little after dark.

Head of Lake Jesup 11 miles from Fort Mellon.
Fort Christmas 37 miles from Fort Mellon, and 12 from Fort Lane on Lake Harney.
Fort McNeil 16 miles from Fort Christmas.
Fort Taylor on Lake Winder – 8 miles from Fort McNeil and estimated to be about 15 miles from the Atlantic and 100 by the river St Johns from Fort Lane.

The Column under Genl Eustis, consisting of the 3rd Regt of Art. 4 Companies of the 4th and the 2nd Dragoons and 4 Companies Alabama Volunteers moved from Fort Mellon on the 17th Decb for the field – a train of 50 Waggons with 20,000 rations moved with it. The column met with obstacles almost insurmountable. On the 25th Decb it reached Fort Christmas. In that distance upwards of twenty bridges from 20 to 70 feet long had to be built, besides a number of causeways – 6 or 7 dense Palmettos or cabbage tree Hummocks from a quarter to ¾ of a mile in depth had to [be cut] through and made passable – pine barriers and scrub cut through. The bush roots or hack cover the [ground] and obstruct the way down. Indeed almost [every] foot of ground for the [entire] distance had to be [prepared] before the column came along. The troops remained [in] camp at Fort Christmas until 3rd Jany. In the mean time the Country around was scoured in every direction. Fort Christmas built 80 feet square of pine pickets with two substantial Block houses 20 feet square – supplies were hauled out from Fort Lane. The Dragoons were sent ahead on 25th to establish Fort McNeil. Fort Taylor established also, and supplies ordered up in boats to that post from Fort Lane under Col Harney. The boats were 4 days in getting [from] Fort Lane to Fort Taylor. On the 28th Capt Winder 2nd Dragoons captured near this post 4 warriors and 24 women and children. They were moving south. We find all the indian Villages which are numerous in this section deserted. The column left Fort Christmas on the 3rd Jany [and] garrisoned that post with 9 Compy 3rd Art under Major Lomax. The difficulties of getting along increased & reached Fort Taylor on the 6th Jany. Genl Jesup has been with the column since it moved from Fort Mellon and I believe has directed all its movements up to the 6th Jany on which day after [having received] intelligence of Col Taylor's battle, he started with 8 Companies of Dragoons to join Col T [Taylor] after getting about 20 miles he sent back an express with instructions to Genl Eustis to make a reconnaissance of the Country more to the west as the route he had taken nearly S.W. was almost impossible for pack horses.

Jany 8th Fort Taylor Capt Fowler with his Dragoons & Lt Anderson sent out to examine the Country. A good wharf built – new and larger pickets jutting up – these put up by the Dragoons just large enough for a store house when roofed. Boats sent down to Fort Lane on the 7th for supplies –

Jany 9th waiting the return of Captn Fowler and Lieut Anderson.

131

The following paragraph would logically seem to follow after the 4th paragraph from the beginning.

From the deck of the steam boat the western shore of the Lake [Harney] near the head appeared to present a very fine position for a Depot. Growth of timber: Live oak and Palmetto with Pine trees. We sent the small boat a couple miles up the St Johns from the bar at the head of the lake, and found plenty of water for light steam boats that distance. Lake Harney is larger & deeper than Lake Monroe — affording from 8 to 18 feet water. The river from Lake Monroe to Lake Harney gives an average depth of about 6 feet. In going up the river and returning, I took the courses and distances with a good pocket compass & time piece, and on my return to Ft Mellon made as correct a map of the river & Lake & the charms of the country, as the means afforded would allow but sufficiently correct however for all practical purposes. This was immediately forwarded to Genl Jesup at Garey's ferry.

Wm. B. Davidson
3rd Arty

The commentary that Davidson penned on the lower right margin is incomplete because this section of the map has been torn off. However, it can be determined from the incomplete sentence remnants that Davidson is telling the same story, the beginning of which he dates November 19, 1837, that Pickell relates in his entries of November 19 to 23. Both Davidson and Pickell mention Colonel Bankhead's command as including themselves together with lieutenants Ringgold, Martin, Taylor, Mock, and Ross on the steamboats Santee *and* McLean, *which had trouble crossing the bars at the heads of lakes Monroe and Harney. They both define the purpose of the mission as to establish a military depot on Lake Harney. Accordingly, the gist of this portion of Davidson's commentary can thus be found in Pickell.*

The following is the bottom left part of the commentary.

In the direction of the river SSE nothing was to be seen but extensive low savannas without a stick of timber, save here and there a few scattering Palmettoes. Here commence the Everglades. The John McKlean [*John McLean, a steamboat*] returned on the 24th with dispatches from General Eustis who sent up a Negro guide "Ben." This negro stated that there was a trail through the Savanna 20 miles above Lake Harney where the indians frequently crossed the St. Johns. Col Bankhead immediately dispatched two Barges under Lieuts Pickell, Ross and Tompkins with Ben to test the truth of the story. Ben was right. They reached the trail which runs by this point where Fort Christmas is built. But they found it impracticable to get supplies from the river over the Savannas and not march two or three miles to the main land. As far as was examined above Lake Harney, and as far as the eye could reach, there was no position thought suitable for a Depot. I considered this western shore of Lake Harney near its head, & where Fort Lane now stands as presenting a very advantageous position for a Depot, but Col Bankhead objected to it, as did also the rest of the Officers, and Genl Eustis if I understood rightly from Col Bankhead who thought it was too near Fort Mellon. The Command returned to Fort Mellon on the 27th Novb with the view of returning as soon as boats could be provisioned, to establish a kind of floating Depot at the head of Lake Harney, or higher up the river. On our return to Fort Mellon, I gave Genl Jesup at his request a sheet of notes, stating all the particulars as to the practicability of establishing a Depot at the head of Lake Harney. He seemed satisfied of the feasibility of doing so, and Major Dearborn has since established a good post.

Rec'd this day from Lieut. W. B. Davidson,
an officer of Artillery – serving with the Army
in Florida.
      R. Jones [Adjutant General]
      Jany, 29th 1838

Notes

CHAPTER ONE

1. James Branch Cabell and Alfred J. Hanna, *The St. Johns,* p. 264.
2. Frank J. Laumer, "This Was Fort Dade," *Florida Historical Quarterly (FHQ)* 45 (July 1966): 11.
3. *Army and Navy Chronicle* 5: 365.
4. *American State Papers: Military Affairs (ASPMA)* 416; John T. Sprague, *The Origin, Progress, and Conclusion of the Florida War,* p. 5.
5. John K. Mahon, "Treaty of Moultrie Creek, 1823," FHQ 40 (April 1962): 369.
6. Charlton W. Tebeau, *A History of Florida,* p. 155.
7. Tebeau, *History,* pp. 1, 6, 16.
8. John Bartram, *Diary of a Journey through the Carolinas, Georgia, and Florida from July 1, 1765, to April 10, 1766,* pp. 41, 72.
9. J. Clarence Simpson, *A Provisional Gazetteer of Florida Place-Names of Indian Derivation,* p. 143.
10. Helen Hornbeck Tanner, *Zéspedes in East Florida,* pp. 142-44, 147.
11. John Bartram, *Diary,* pp. 43, 73, and plate 7.
12. Charles Vignoles, *Observations Upon the Floridas,* pp. 66, 68-69. This reference was supplied by Dr. Dorothy Dodd.
13. John Bartram, *Diary,* pp. 42, 43, 73, and plate 7.
14. *Ibid.,* pp. 41, 42, 72, and plate 7.
15. Sprague, *Florida War,* pp. 259, 327.

CHAPTER TWO

1. Jacob Rhett Motte, *Journey into Wilderness,* p. 273.
2. John M. Goggin, "Osceola: Portraits, Features, and Dress," *FHQ* 33 (January and April 1955): 162-63, 166-67; "Portraits of Osceola and the Artists Who Painted Them," *Papers of the Jacksonville Historical Society* 2 (1949): 37-39.
3. John T. Sprague, "Journal Kept in Florida during the Months of April and May, 1839," manuscript.
4. Motte, *Journey,* p. 101.
5. J. N. Whitner, "Sanford History," mimeographed, p. 10.
6. Motte, *Journey,* p. 276.
7. Harry T. Peters, *America on Stone,* pp. 199-200.
8. Unlike the products of later and better-known firms, the two Greene & McGowran lithographs were never hailed as shining lights, a fact that might be attributed to public apathy rather than to artistic shortcomings. At least Greene & McGowran's 30 Wall Street address brought the company close to fame – next door to where George Washington had made his first inaugural address forty-eight years earlier. See *American Prints, 1813-1913.*
9. "Orders of the Army of the South" 19: order 10.
10. *Florida Conservation News* 11, no. 5 (February 1976): 2.
11. Washington Irving, *The Adventures of Captain Bonneville, U.S.A.* (New York, 1881), p. 86.

12. Captain Electus Backus, "Diary of a Campaign in Florida, in 1837-8," *Historical Magazine*, September 1866, pp. 279-85.
13. *Niles' National Register* 54: 273: "Post Returns for Fort Mellon," December 1837.

CHAPTER THREE

1. J. H. Eaton, comp., "Returns of Killed and Wounded in Battles or Engagements with the Indians, British, and Mexican Troops, 1790-1848": Jesup to Fanning, March 6, 1837, and Fenwick to Poinsett, July 9, 1840; *House Documents* 78: 65.
2. Sprague, *Florida War*, pp. xxi, xxii.
3. Edwin C. McReynolds, *The Seminoles*, p. 231.
4. Motte, *Journey*, pp. xiv, xv, 94.
5. Logan U. Reavis, *The Life and Military Services of General William Selby Harney*, p. 101; "Orders of the Army of the South" 19: order 36.
6. John Lee Williams, *The Territory of Florida*, p. 269.
7. Williams, *Territory*, p. 269; Motte, *Journey*, pp. 8, 251; ASPMA 893
8. *Niles' Weekly Register* 52: 31-32; Sprague, *Florida War*, pp. 168-70, 319, 325; Williams, *Territory*, pp. 268-69; Motte, *Journey*, pp. 100-101, 102-4; Reavis, *Harney*, pp. 102-4; Whitner, "Sanford History," p. 9; *House Documents* 78: 67.
9. "Recollections of Coacoochee," *The Daily Georgian* (Savannah), February 19, 1842.
10. Eaton, "Returns": Fanning to Jesup, February 11 and 12, 1837; *House Documents* 78: 72-73.
11. Sprague, *Florida War*, p. 168; Joshua R. Giddings, *The Exiles of Florida*, p. 136; Theophilus Francis Rodenbough, *From Everglade to Canyon with the Second Dragoons*, p. 24; Eaton, "Returns": Jesup to Fanning, March 6, 1837.
12. Whitner, "Sanford History," p. 9; Sidney Walter Martin, *Florida During the Territorial Days*, p. 236; Charles Henry Coe, *Red Patriots*, p. 126; Giddings, *Exiles*, p. 291.

CHAPTER FOUR

1. *ASPMA* 866; Eaton, "Returns": Jesup to Fanning, March 6, 1837.
2. Sprague, *Florida War*, pp. 177-78; Coe, *Red Patriots*, pp. 14-15, 74; John K. Mahon, *History of the Second Seminole War*, pp. 200-201.
3. Both Lake Poinsett, in the northwest corner of Brevard County, and the poinsettia are named after Joel Poinsett.
4. *ASPMA* 871.
5. Sprague, *Florida War*, p. 178; Williams, *Territory*, p. 270; Mark F. Boyd, "Asi Yaholo, or Osceola," *FHQ* 33 (January and April 1955): 249-305; ASPMA 870-71; *Niles' Weekly Register* 52: 213.
6. Francis Parkman, *The Conspiracy of Pontiac and the Indian War after the Conquest of Canada*, p. 286; *Fort Michilimackinac Sketch Book*, pp. 30-34.
7. *ASPMA* 871.
8. Williams, *Territory*, p. 237.
9. Simpson, *Gazetteer*, p. 26.
10. Giddings, *Exiles*, p. 155; Sprague, *Florida War*, p. 196.
11. Giddings, *Exiles*, pp. 145, 148, 151-54.
12. *Ibid.*, p. 164.

13. Laumer, "This Was Fort Dade," p. 9.
14. Motte, *Journey*, pp. 94, 99; Sprague, *Florida War*, pp. 257, 273.
15. Motte, *Journey*, p. 100.
16. *Ibid.*, p. 104; William Bartram, *Travels Through North and South Carolina, Georgia, East and West Florida*, p. 398.
17. Motte, *Journey*, pp. 104, 105; Sprague, *Florida War*, pp. 169, 526.
18. *Niles' National Register* 56: 386; Coe, *Red Patriots*, p. 267; John T. Sprague, "Macomb's Mission to the Seminoles," *FHQ* 35 (October 1956): 148; Francis B. Heitman, *Historical Register and Dictionary of the United States Army*, p. 514; H. J. Chaffer, "Florida Forts Established Prior to 1860," typescript.
19. Cabell and Hanna, *The St. Johns*, p. 195; Sprague, *Florida War*, p. 224.
20. William Fremont Blackman, *The History of Orange County, Florida*, pp. 19, 73.
21. ASPMA 845.
22. Motte, *Journey*, p. 105; *Niles' Weekly Register* 52: 289; ASPMA 845; *Army and Navy Chronicle* 5: 187; *House Documents* 78: 101.

CHAPTER FIVE

1. ASPMA 839, 844, 845; *House Documents* 78: 102.
2. ASPMA 837, 866, 878; *House Documents* 78: 161, 171.
3. Williams, *Territory*, p. 55.
4. Jack C. Rosenau and Glen L. Faulkner, "An Index to Springs of Florida," pamphlet.
5. John Bartram, *Diary*, pp. 42, 73.
6. Motte, *Journey*, pp. 114, 250.
7. Williams, *Territory*, p. iv; ASPMA 867; *House Documents* 219: 6.
8. The Captain Poinsett mentioned in this extract may be the Captain Poinsett whom Mueller identifies as master of the steamer *George Washington*, active in 1834.
9. Sprague, *Florida War*, p. 192; Army map L247-2, "Téatre of Military Operations in Florida during 1835, 36, & 37." (A copy of this map has been donated to the Henry Shelton Sanford Library Museum in Sanford.)
10. Army map L247-2.
11. Cabell and Hanna, *The St. Johns*, pp. 263, 264.
12. Williams, *Territory*, p. iv.
13. Sprague, *Florida War*, p. 192; ASPMA 890; Reavis, *Harney*, p. 474.

CHAPTER SIX

1. Coe, *Red Patriots*, p. 93; Gary E. Moulton, "Cherokees and the Second Seminole War," *FHQ* 53 (January 1975): 296.
2. Grant Foreman, *Indian Removal*, p. 2; Coe, *Red Patriots*, pp. 93-94.
3. Foreman, *Indian Removal*, p. 532; Grant Foreman, ed., "Report of the Cherokee Deputies in Florida, February 17, 1838, to John Ross, Esq.," *Chronicles of Oklahoma* 9 (December 1931): 438; Motte, *Journey*, pp. 149-50.
4. Coe, *Red Patriots*, p. 95.
5. Foreman, "Report," p. 427.
6. *Ibid.*, p. 428; Sprague, *Florida War*, p. 191.
7. Moulton, "Cherokees," pp. 297, 298, 300; ASPMA 816, 853, 854; Poinsett to Jesup,

October 13, 1837, in *House Documents* 78: 122.

8. Foreman, "Report," pp. 427, 428; Simpson, *Gazetteer*, p. 116; Motte, *Journey*, p. 166; *Army and Navy Chronicle* 5: 382; *The Sentinel Star* (Orlando), June 15, 1976.
9. Foreman, "Report," p. 429.
10. Foreman, *Indian Removal*, p. 353; Coe, *Red Patriots*, p. 95; Boyd, "Asi Yaholo," p. 300.
11. Moulton, "Cherokees," p. 298. See also Coe, *Red Patriots*, p. 95; Boyd, "Asi Yaholo," p. 300.
12. Foreman, "Report," p. 431.
13. *Ibid.* See also Sprague, *Florida War*, p. 191.
14. Sprague, *Florida War*, pp. 99, 270; Motte, *Journey*, p. 283.
15. Foreman, "Report," p. 431.
16. *Ibid.*, p. 433.
17. *Ibid.*, p. 435.
18. *Ibid.*, p. 434.
19. *Ibid.*, pp. 434-35.
20. *Ibid.*, p. 434; Motte, *Journey*, p. 170.
21. Foreman, "Report," p. 436.
22. *Ibid.*, p. 437.
23. Moulton, "Cherokees," p. 304.
24. Sprague, *Florida War*, p. 191.
25. ASPMA 894

CHAPTER SEVEN

1. *House Documents* 78: 197.
2. *The News* (St. Augustine), May 14, 1839.
3. John H. Goff, "The Steamboat Period in Georgia," *Georgia Historical Quarterly* 12 (September 1928): 242-43; Edward A. Mueller, "East Coast Florida Steamboating 1831-1861," *FHQ* 40 (January 1962): 242, 244, 251, 253, 256.
4. ASPMA 835-36, 877; *Army and Navy Chronicle* 5: 381.
5. Motte, *Journey*, p. 98; Sprague, *Florida War*, p. 148.
6. Williams, *Territory*, p. 271; *Niles' Weekly Register* 52: 289; Sprague, *Florida War*, p. 192.
7. ASPMA 811.
8. *Ibid.*, p. 877; George E. Buker, *Swamp Sailors*, p. 43.
9. ASPMA 994-96; Mueller, "Steamboating," pp. 242-49; William M. Lytle, *Merchant Steam Vessels of the United States 1806-1868*, pp. 25, 30, 32, 66, 102, 171, 220.
10. Lytle, *Merchant Steam Vessels*, pp. 25, 30, 32, 66, 102, 171, 220.
11. Edward A. Mueller, "East Coast Florida Steamboating 1831-1861," typescript.
12. *Army and Navy Chronicle* 5: 381.
13. M. M. Cohen, *Notices of Florida and the Campaign*, pp. 109, 113, 115, 123; Williams, *Territory*, p. 260; ASPMA 994-96; Mueller, "Steamboating," p. 246; *Niles' National Register* 53: 273.
14. Sprague, *Florida War*, p. 246; Lytle, *Merchant Steam Vessels*, p. 171.
15. Goff, "Steamboat Period," p. 253; Lytle, *Merchant Steam Vessels*, pp. 30, 32, 66, 102, 220; Alfred J. Hanna, *Fort Maitland*, p. 71.
16. Motte, *Journey*, p. 95; Letter of July 13, 1839, in DeGrange Index, Record Group 77, National Archives; Williams, *Territory*, pp. 248-50, 260.
17. Mueller, "East Coast Florida Steamboating" and "Louis Mitchell Coxetter," typescripts.
18. *Army and Navy Chronicle* 5: 382; Mueller, "Steamboating," p. 245.
19. Buker, *Swamp Sailors*, pp. 42-43.

20. ASPMA 877.
21. John K. Mahon, *The War of 1812*, p. 253.

CHAPTER EIGHT

1. ASPMA 278, 435; Cohen, *Notices*, pp. 216-17; Chaffer, "Florida Forts."
2. John Bartram, *Diary*, pp. 43, 73.
3. Cabell and Hanna, *The St. Johns*, p. 195.
4. ASPMA 873.
5. Sprague, *Florida War*, p. 188; "Orders of the Army of the South" 19: order 10.
6. Motte, *Journey*, p. 146.
7. Mahon, *Second Seminole War*, pp. 219-20.
8. Sprague, *Florida War*, p. 188.
9. "Orders of the Army of the South" 19: order 10; Sprague, *Florida War*, pp. 188-91; ASPMA 887.
10. Sprague, *Florida War*, p. 104; Mahon, *Second Seminole War*, p. 225.
11. Mahon, *Second Seminole War*, p. 226.
12. Sprague, *Florida War*, p. 192; *Niles' National Register* 55: 30-31, and 53: 273.
13. ASPMA 893-94.
14. *Ibid.*, p. 893.
15. *Ibid.*, p. 894; Mahon, *Second Seminole War*, p. 231; Army map L247-2.
16. Samuel Forry, "Letters of Samuel Forry, Surgeon, U.S. Army, 1837, '38," *FHQ* 7 (July 1928): 98; Sprague, "Macomb's Mission," p. 148.
17. "Post Returns for Fort Lane"; Motte, *Journey*, p. 261.
18. Pleasant Daniel Gold, *History of Volusia County, Florida*, p. 73; Coe, *Red Patriots*, p. 267; Heitman, *Register*, p. 516; *Niles' National Register* 56: 386.
19. Mahon, *Second Seminole War*, pp. 231, 233; Army map L247-2; ASPMA 894.
20. William and Ellen Hartly, *Osceola*, p. 255.
21. Motte, *Journey*, p. 300.
22. Rodenbough, *Everglade*, pp 28-31.
23. Maurice Matloff, ed., *American Military History*, p. 160; Williams, *Territory*, p. 266.
24. *Centennial of the United States Military Academy at West Point, New York, 1802-1902* 1: 535.
25. "Returns from U.S. Military Posts 1800-1916," pamphlet, pp. 1, 3.
26. "Orderbook of Gen. Thomas S. Jesup, January 29 to May 22, 1838," manuscript.
27. "Post Returns for Fort Gatlin," November 1838-June 1839 and October 1849.
28. Sprague, *Florida War*, pp. 233-34; McReynolds, *The Seminoles*, pp. 219-20.
29. Nathaniel Wyche Hunter, "Captain Nathaniel Wyche Hunter and the Florida Indian Campaigns 1837-1841," *FHQ* 39 (July 1960): 66; "Orderbook of General Jesup, 1838."
30. Sprague, *Florida War*, pp. 305, 308.
31. *Ibid.*, p. 483.
32. Thomas H. S. Hamersley, comp. and ed., *Complete Regular Army Register of the United States*, p. 145.

CHAPTER NINE

1. Allen Morris, *The Florida Handbook 1975-1976*, pp. 74, 78; Herbert J. Doherty, Jr., *Richard Keith Call*, p. 124.
2. Letter from Governor Reid to Secretary of War Poinsett, August 22, 1840, in *Territorial Papers of the United States* 26: xxvi, 202-4.
3. "Orders of the Army of the South" 11-12: order 82.
4. Tebeau, *History*, p. 225.
5. Sprague, *Florida War*, pp. 526-29; Sidney Lanier, *Florida*, p. 130.
6. Gold, *Volusia County*, p. 73; Mahon, *Second Seminole War*, pp. 161, 272.
7. Whitner, "Sanford History," p. 11.
8. "Orders of the Army of the South" 11-12.
9. *Ibid.*; "Letters Received 1780's-1917," Adjutant General's Office, T43.
10. "Letters," T22, T23.
11. *Ibid.*, T22.
12. *Ibid.*, T21.
13. *Ibid.*, A132.
14. Whitner, "Sanford History," p. 13.
15. George M. Barbour, *Florida for Tourists, Invalids, and Settlers*, p. 121; Heitman, *Register*, p. 537.
16. Gold, *Volusia County*, p. 64.
17. Whitner, "Sanford History," p. 13.
18. Gold, *Volusia County*, pp. 71-72, 83.
19. Blackman, *Orange County*, pp. 25, 49, 51, 94, 198, 204; Whitner, "Sanford History," pp. 18, 20.
20. Margaret Barnes, "Field Notes," typescript, p. 4; Whitner, "Sanford History," p. 23; Barbour, *Florida for Tourists*, p. 120.
21. Mahon, *Second Seminole War*, p. 253.

CHAPTER TEN

1. T. A. Mellon, "Captain Charles Mellon," *FHQ* 15 (April 1937): 281.
2. *Ibid.*; Cohen, *Notices*, p. 84; Williams, *Territory*, pp. 221, 222; John Bemrose, *Reminiscences of the Second Seminole War*, p. 49.
3. Motte, *Journey*, p. 101; *Army and Navy Chronicle* 5: 89; Sprague, "Macomb's Mission," p. 148.
4. Sprague, *Florida War, p. 525;* Whitner, "Sanford History," pp. 8-9.
5. A copy of Mellon's speech is in the Fort Mellon vertical file at Mills Memorial Library, Rollins College.
6. *House Reports* 378 and 447.
7. Sprague, *Florida War*, pp. 168, 392; Motte, *Journey*, pp. 103-4; Heitman, *Register*, p. 954; George Washington Cullum, *Biographical Register of the Officers and Graduates of the U.S. Military Academy 1802-1890*, p. 654; *Centennial of the U.S. Military Academy*, p. 543.
8. Motte, *Journey*, p. 155; Mahon, *Second Seminole War*, pp. 289, 323; Sprague, *Florida War*, p. 246.
9. ASPMA 888.
10. *Centennial of the U.S. Military Academy*, p. 543; Goggin, "Osceola," p. 162; Forry, "Letters," pp. 97-98; Cullum, *Biographical Register*, pp. 159-60; ASPMA 888; Williams, *Territory*, pp. 285-86; *National Cyclopaedia of American Biography* 9: 370-71.

11. Hanna, *Fort Maitland*, pp. 71-73; Bemrose, *Reminiscences*, pp. 26, 30, 32, 50; Cohen, *Notices*, pp. 55, 65; Heitman, *Register*, pp. 412-13; *Centennial of the U.S. Military Academy*, p. 538; Cullum, *Biographical Register*, pp. 107-8.
12. Rodenbough, *Everglade*, pp. 19-21, 24.
13. Reavis, *Harney*, pp. 35, 39, 44, 91; Rodenbough, *Everglade*, pp. 24, 436; Heitman, *Register*, p. 502; Mahon, *Second Seminole War*, pp. 261-62.
14. Heitman, *Register*, p. 614; Rodenbough, *Everglade*, pp. 448-49; Mahon, *Second Seminole War*, pp. 173, 182.
15. Rodenbough, *Everglade*, pp. 431, 439; Heitman, *Register*, p. 173; Sprague, *Florida War*, pp. 218-19, 224; Williams, *Territory*, p. 247; Cohen, *Notices*, p. 160.
16. Rodenbough, *Everglade*, p. 449; Heitman, *Register*, p. 1049.
17. Motte, *Journey*, pp. 117-23; 130, 280; Rodenbough, *Everglade*, pp. 20, 431, 482; *Centennial of the U.S. Military Academy*, p. 583; Heitman, *Register*, p. 679; ASPMA 849-50.
18. Rodenbough, *Everglade*, p. 490; Heitman, *Register*, p. 601; Motte, *Journey*, p. 104.
19. Rodenbough, *Everglade*, p. 450; Heitman, *Register*, p. 468; Cohen, *Notices*, p. 237; Bemrose, *Reminiscences*, p. 21; Cullum, *Biographical Register*, pp. 585-86; ASPMA 849; Warren G. Fouraker, "The Administtret on of Robert Raymond Reid," master's thesis.
20. Rodenbough, *Everglade*, pp. 28, 436, 449, 450; *Niles' National Register* 53: 240.
21. Heitman, *Register*, pp. 203, 493, 547-48.
22. Eaton, "Returns": Clinch to Jones, January 2, 1837.
23. Williams, *Territory*, p. 55; Motte, *Journey*, pp. 116, 121; Heitman, *Register*, p. 787; Cullum, *Biographical Register*, pp. 472-73.
24. Motte, *Journey*, p. 274; Heitman, *Register*, p. 356; Cullum, *Biographical Register*, pp. 143-44; *Centennial of the U.S. Military Academy*, p. 544.
25. Cullum, *Biographical Register*, p. 285; Letter of John Pickell January 16, 1844, and letter of commissioner to surveyor general, February 23, 1844, in General Land Office Records, Record Group 49, National Archives.
26. *Register of Graduates and Former Cadets United States Military Academy, 1802-1949*; "Post Returns of Fort Mellon."
27. Sprague, *Florida War*, pp. 200, 167; *Centennial of the U.S. Military Academy*, p. 545.
28. Hanna, *Fort Maitland*, p. 65; Mahon, *Second Seminole War*, p. 193; Motte, *Journey*, p. 137; Sprague, *Florida War*, pp. 167, 193, 194, 200; Frank E. Snyder and Brian H. Guss, *The District: A History of the Philadelphia District U.S. Army Corps of Engineers, 1866-1971* (Philadelphia: U.S. Army Engineer District, 1974), p. 11.
29. Cohen, *Notices*, pp. 109, 113, 204, 227; Bemrose, *Reminiscences*, pp. 81-82; Sprague, *Florida War*, pp. 192-193, 194; ASPMA 893; Motte, *Journey*, p. 188; Backus, "Diary," p. 284; Mahon, *Second Seminole War*, p. 164; Allen Morris, *Florida Place Names*, p. 53.
30. Mahon, *Second Seminole War*, pp. 99, 102, 135; Williams, *Territory*, p. xi; Motte, *Journey*, p. 178; ASPMA 890.

CHAPTER ELEVEN

1. *Sanford Herald*, February 8, 1937.
2. Henry S. Sanford may have exaggerated when he spoke of the city named in his honor as the "Gate City of South Florida." With the advent of the Auto-Train, however, Sanford is again an important point of entry.
3. Morris, *Florida Handbook*, p. 403.
4. Rodenbough, *Everglade*, p. 82.
5. ASPMA 832; Jesup to Butler in *House Documents* 78: 75.
6. William Bartram, *Travels*, p. 26.
7. Hunter, "Captain Nathaniel Hunter," p. 73-74.

Bibliography

American Prints, 1813-1913. Catalog prepared by the Department of Prints and Drawings, Boston Museum of Fine Arts. April 12-15, 1975.

American State Papers. Vol. 2: *Indian Affairs.* Washington, 1832-34. Vol. 7: *Military Affairs.* Washington, 1832-60.

Army and Navy Chronicle. Washington, 1835-42.

Army map L247-1. Civil Works Map File, Record Group 77, National Archives. (This map shows army deployments and Seminole positions for September 1837.)

Army map L247-2. Office of the Chief of Engineers, Record Group 77, National Archives. (This map shows the theater of military operations in Florida for the years 1835-37. The right and bottom margins offer a commentary in minuscule script by Lieutenant Davidson.)

Army map L247-4. Office of the Chief of Engineers, Record Group 77, National Archives. (This map was drawn up by order of General Taylor in 1839.)

Backus, Capt. Electus. "Diary of a Campaign in Florida, in 1837-8." *Historical Magazine,* September 1866, 279-85.

Barbour, George M. *Florida for Tourists, Invalids, and Settlers.* 1882. Reprint. Gainesville: The University Presses of Florida, 1964.

Barnes, Margaret. "Field Notes." Federal Writers' Project, July 8, 1936. Typescript in the P. K. Yonge Library of Florida History, Gainesville.

Bartram, John. *Diary of a Journey through the Carolinas, Georgia, and Florida from July 1, 1765, to April 10, 1766.* Edited by Francis Harper. Reprinted from *Transactions of the American Philosophical Society,* new series, vol. 33, part 1. December 1942.

Bartram, William. *Travels Through North and South Carolina, Georgia, East and West Florida.* Edited by Mark van Doren. New York, 1955.

Bemrose, John. *Reminiscences of the Second Seminole War.* Edited by John K. Mahon. Gainesville: The University Presses of Florida, 1966.

Blackman, William Fremont. *The History of Orange County, Florida.* 1927. Reprint. Chuluota: The Mickler House, 1973.

Boyd, Mark F. "Asi Yaholo, or Osceola." *Florida Historical Quarterly* 33 (January and April 1955): 249-305.

Buker, George E. *Swamp Sailors: Riverine Warfare in the Everglades 1835-1842.* Gainesville: The University Presses of Florida, 1975.

Cabell, James Branch, and Hanna, Alfred J. *The St. Johns: A Parade of Diversities.* New York, 1943.

Centennial of the United States Military Academy at West Point, New York, 1802-1902. Vol. 1. Washington: Government Printing Office, 1904.

Chaffer, H. J. "Florida Forts Established Prior to 1860." Typescript in the P. K. Yonge Library of Florida History, Gainesville.

Coe, Charles Henry. *Red Patriots: The Story of the Seminoles.* 1898. Reprint. Gainesville: The University Presses of Florida, 1974.

Cohen, M. M. *Notices of Florida and the Campaigns.* 1836. Reprint. Gainesville: The University Presses of Florida, 1964.

Cullum, George Washington. *Biographical Register of the Officers and Graduates of the United States Military Academy. . . 1802-1890.* 3 vols. Boston, 1891.

Davidson, William B. "Map of Fort Mellon, Florida." November 10, 1837. Adjutant General's Office, Record Group 94, National Archives.

Eaton, J. H., comp. "Returns of Killed and Wounded in Battles or Engagements with the Indians, British, and Mexican Troops, 1790-1848." 1850-51. Manuscript in the Military Archives Division, Navy and Old Army Branch, National Archives.

Foreman, Grant. *Indian Removal: The Emigration of the Five Civilized Tribes of Indians.* Norman: University of Oklahoma Press, 1953.

————— , ed. "Report of the Cherokee Deputies in Florida, February 17, 1838, to John Ross, Esq." *Chronicles of Oklahoma* 9 (December 1931): 423-38.

Forry, Samuel. "Letters of Samuel Forry, Surgeon, U.S. Army, 1837, '38." *Florida Historical Quarterly* 6 (January and April 1928): 206-19; *Florida Historical Quarterly* 7 (July 1928): 88-105.

Fort Mellon vertical file. Mills Memorial Library, Rollins College. (A loose collection of papers and notes apparently accumulated by Alfred J. Hanna.)

Fort Michilimackinac Sketch Book. Mackinac Island: Mackinac Island State Park Commission, 1975.

Fouraker, Warren G. "The Administration of Robert Raymond Reid." Master's thesis, Florida State University, 1949.

Fundaburk, Emma L., ed. *Southeastern Indians: Life Portraits.* Luverne (Alabama): Emma L. Fundaburk, 1958.

Gentry, Daniel E. "Orange County's Forgotten Fort – Fort McNeil." *Orange County Historical Quarterly,* vol. 2, no. 4, December 1969. (This article includes a partial transcription of Lieutenant Davidson's commentary on army map L247-2.)

[Gentry, Daniel E.?] "St. Johns Passage." *Orlando Sentinel Sun, Florida Magazine,* July 29, 1956. (Another partial transcription of Lieutenant Davidson's L247-2 commentary.)

Giddings, Joshua R. *The Exiles of Florida, or, The Crimes Committed by Our Government Against the Maroons, Who Fled from South Carolina and Other Slave States, Seeking Protection Under Spanish Law.* 1858. Reprint. Gainesville: The University Presses of Florida, 1964.

Goff, John H. "The Steamboat Period in Georgia," *Georgia Historical Quarterly* 12 (September 1928): 236-54.

Goggin, John M. "Osceola: Portraits, Features, and Dress." *Florida Historical Quarterly* 33 (January and April 1955): 161-92.

Gold, Pleasant Daniel. *History of Volusia County, Florida.* DeLand: The E. O. Painter Printing Company, 1927.

Hamersley, Thomas Holdup Stevens, comp. and ed. *Complete Regular Army Register of the United States: For One Hundred Years (1779-1879).* Washington, 1880.

Hanna, Alfred J. *Fort Maitland: Its Origin and History.* Maitland, 1936.

Hartly, William and Ellen. *Osceola: The Unconquered Indian.* New York, 1973.

Heitman, Francis B. *Historical Register and Dictionary of the United States Army . . . to March 2, 1903.* 2 vols *(House Documents* 446). Washington: Government Printing Office, 1903. Facsimile reprint. Urbana: University of Illinois Press, 1965.

House Documents 78 and 219, 25th Congress, 2nd session, March 12, 1838.

House Reports 378 and 447, 30th Congress, 1st session, March 30, 1848.

Hunter, Nathaniel Wyche. "Captain Nathaniel Wyche Hunter and the Florida Indian Campaigns, 1837-1841." Edited by Reynold M. Wik. *Florida Historical Quarterly* 39 (July 1960): 62-75.

Lanier, Sidney. *Florida: Its Scenery, Climate, and History.* 1875. Reprint. Gainesville: The University Presses of Florida, 1973.

Laumer, Frank J. "This Was Fort Dade." *Florida Historical Quarterly* 45 (July 1966): 1-11.

"Letters Received 1780's-1917." Adjutant General's Office, Record Group 94, National Archives.

Lytle, William M. *Merchant Steam Vessels of the United States 1806-1868.* Mystic (Connecticut): Steamboat Historical Society of America, 1952.

McCarthy, Joseph E. "Portraits of Osceola and the Artists Who Painted Them." *Papers of the Jacksonville Historical Society* 2 (1949): 23-44.

McReynolds, Edwin C. *The Seminoles.* Norman: University of Oklahoma Press, 1957.

Mahon, John K. *History of the Second Seminole War 1835-1842.* Gainesville: The University Presses of Florida, 1967.

———. "Treaty of Moultrie Creek, 1823." *Florida Historical Quarterly* 40 (April 1962): 350-72.

Martin, Sidney Walter. *Florida During the Territorial Days.* Athens: University of Georgia Press, 1944.

Matloff, Maurice, gen. ed. *American Military History.* Washington: Office of the Chief of Military History, 1969.

Mellon, T. A. "Captain Charles Mellon." *Florida Historical Quarterly.* 15 (April 1937): 281-83.

Morris, Allen. *The Florida Handbook 1975-1976.* Tallahassee: The Peninsular Publishing Company, 1975.

———. *Florida Place Names.* Coral Gables: University of Miami Press, 1974.

Motte, Jacob Rhett. *Journey into Wilderness: An Army Surgeon's Account of Life in Camp and Field During the Creek and Seminole Wars, 1836-1838.* Edited by James F. Sunderman. Gainesville: The University Presses of Florida, 1953.

Moulton, Gary E. "Cherokees and The Second Seminole War." *Florida Historical Quarterly* 53 (January 1975): 296-305.

Mueller, Edward A. "East Coast Florida Steamboating 1831-1861." *Florida Historical Quarterly* 40 (January 1962): 241-60.

Niles' National Register. Baltimore, 1837-49.

Niles' Weekly Register. Baltimore, 1811-37.

"Orderbook of Gen. Thomas S. Jesup, January 29 to May 22, 1838." Manuscript in the P. K. Yonge Library of Florida History, Gainesville.

"Orders of the Army of the South." Adjutant General's Office, Record Group 94, vols. 11-12 and 19, National Archives.

Parkman, Francis. *The Conspiracy of Pontiac and the Indian War after the Conquest of Canada.* Boston, 1913.

Peters, Harry T. *America on Stone: the other printmakers to the American people.* Garden City (New York), 1931.

Peyton, Richard A. "Map of Fort Mellon, Florida." n.d. Adjutant General's Office, Record Group 94, National Archives.

Pickell, John. "John Pickell Papers." Manuscript (Reel 17) in the Library of Congress.

———. "The Journals of Lieutenant John Pickell, 1836-1837." Edited by Frank L. White, Jr. *Florida Historical Quarterly* 38 (October 1959): 142-71.

"Post Returns for Fort Gatlin." November 1838-June 1839 and October 1849. Adjutant General's Office, Record Group 94, Microcopy 617 (Roll 1511), National Archives.

"Post Returns for Fort Lane." December 1837-February 1838. Adjutant General's Office, Record Group 94, Microcopy 617 (Roll 1518), National Archives.

"Post Returns for Fort Mellon." March 1837-April 1842. Adjutant General's Office, Record Group 94, Microcopy 617 (Roll 768), National Archives.

"Post Returns for Fort Reid." July 1840-January 1841. Adjutant General's Office, Record Group 94, Microcopy 617 (Roll 1536), National Archives.

Reavis, Logan U. *The Life and Military Services of General William Selby Harney.* St. Louis, 1878.

Register of Graduates and Former Cadets United States Military Academy, 1802-1949. New York: West Point Alumni Foundation, 1949.

"Returns from U.S. Military Posts 1800-1916." Pamphlet accompanying Microcopy 617. Washington: National Archives Microfilm Publication, 1968.

Rodenbough, Theophilus Francis. *From Everglade to Canyon with the Second Dragoons.* New York, 1875.

Rosenau, Jack C., and Faulkner, Glen L. "An Index to Springs of Florida." United States Geological Survey in cooperation with Bureau of Geology, Florida Department of Natural Resources. Tallahassee, 1974.

St. Augustine News. May 4, 1839.

Sanford Herald. February 8 and 9, 1937; April 26, 1963.

Simpson, J. Clarence. *A Provisional Gazetteer of Florida Place-Names of Indian Derivation.* Edited by Mark F. Boyd. Tallahassee: Florida Board of Conservation (Special Publication 1), 1956.

Sprague, John T. "Macomb's Mission to the Seminoles: John T. Sprague's Journal Kept During April and May, 1839." Edited by Frank L. White, Jr. *Florida Historical Quarterly* 35 (October 1956): 130-93.

———. Manuscript of above "Journal." Joseph M. Toner Papers, Box 269, The Library of Congress.

———. *The Origin, Progress, and Conclusion of the Florida War.* 1848. Reprint. Gainesville: The University Presses of Florida, 1964.

Tanner, Helen Hornbeck. *Zéspedes in East Florida.* Coral Gables: University of Miami Press, 1963.

Tebeau, Charlton W. *A History of Florida.* Coral Gables: University of Miami Press, 1971.
Territorial Papers of the United States. Vol. 26: *The Territory of Florida, 1839-48.* Edited by C. E. Carter. 1962. National Archives.
Vignoles, Charles. *Observations Upon the Floridas.* New York, 1823.
Whitner, J. N. "Sanford History," 1910. Mimeographed. Sanford Public Library, 1952.
Williams, John Lee. *The Territory of Florida.* 1837. Reprint. Gainesville: The University Presses of Florida, 1962.

Index

146

147

Chief Bugler - Sergt Major. 1844

148